How to Sell: Recipes for Retail

How to Sell: Recipes for Retail

The fine art of getting just the right mix of ingredients to delight customers

John Hoerner

EBURY
PRESS

1 3 5 7 9 10 8 6 4 2

Ebury Press, an imprint of Ebury Publishing,
20 Vauxhall Bridge Road,
London, SW1V 2SA

Ebury Press is part of the Penguin Random House group
of companies whose addresses can be found at
global.penguinrandomhouse.com

Penguin
Random House
UK

First published by Ebury Press in 2015

www.eburypublishing.co.uk

An edition of this book was first published by Guangdong Economic
Press in Chinese and English language in July 2015, under the title
Recipes For Retailers. This edition is published in agreement with
Guangdong Economic Press.

A CIP catalogue record for this book is available from
the British Library

ISBN: 9781785032837

Typeset ... Pvt Ltd, Noida, D... i

Printed a... d bound in Great Britain by Clays Ltd, St Ives ... LC

Penguin Ra... ... e for
our business, our readers and our planet. This book is ma... from
F...

Praise for *How To Sell* from industry experts

'This book epitomises John's approach to business, short, simple, entertaining and above all effective. His great achievement during his long career has been his ability to teach others and this book now enables more to learn from his experience.'

Richard Brasher, Chief Executive of Pick & Pay, Cape Town,
former Chief Executive of Tesco UK

'A "Master Class" for retailers . . . it's good, thought-provoking stuff and will become an essential reference guide to management excellence. John's achievements in business are a matter of public record; his impact on countless aspiring executives is less well known, but treasured by them all.'

Mike Goring, Operations Director of Debenhams,
former Operations Director of Arcadia Group

'Every budding executive needs a mentor to help develop your skills, support you through difficult times and allow you the room to learn from your mistakes. Mentoring is just one of the recipes John Hoerner has honed throughout his half a century in retail, and one I was fortunate to benefit from. [This book] will give everyone the chance to learn from his experience. It is a book I wish I had written!'

Terry Green, Retail Consultant, former Chief Executive of
Top Shop, Debenhams, BHS, Allders and Tesco Clothing

'John Hoerner makes many of the issues we battle daily in retail seem so simple and straightforward. That takes many years of insight. I recommend that you could save yourself a few years of retail learning pain by reading this book.'

Neela Montgomery, Chairwoman of Crate & Barrel,
Member of the Board for Multichannel Retail, Otto Group

'I had the privilege of working with John Hoerner for ten years at Tesco. He always amazed me with the way he approached any situation, looking at solutions from surprising angles that I had not considered.
I practised most of the advice John gives in his book and it does work. In fact it is so simple and common sense, you'll wish you had thought of it yourself.'

Christophe Roussel, International Sourcing Consultant,
former Head of Tesco International Sourcing

'John Hoerner has been an inspiration for many generations of retailers who have had the privilege of working with him. I consider him to be the architect of the modern Debenhams. I believe this book will become an essential read for anyone in retail or anyone who wants to understand retailing better. Retailing is a competitive, fast-moving business and this book covers all of the key ingredients which any successful retailer needs to consider. I wholeheartedly recommend it.'

Mike Sharp, CEO of Debenhams Department Stores

'I've known John since he joined Tesco in 2001 and I've either worked for him or with him (which is much the same thing) almost ever since. There is never a dull moment let alone a dull conversation and I have learnt more from John than almost anyone else, much of it covered in this book. Read it to short-cut your retail education. I thoroughly recommend this book – it contains much of the wisdom I have gained from John in the last 13 years I have known him. I must say it reads much like most of the conversations I've had with John over the years, i.e. don't expect a comfortable read and reassuring sound bites – John has always been a dispenser of tough love and truth, not feel-good theory – but at the end of it you will have learnt a lot and be better for having read it.'

Jason Tarry, Commercial Director of Tesco UK and International

'I learnt more from John alone than all others, collectively, that I have encountered put together in my 30+ years in retail. He has made a huge impact on UK retail, most particularly by grabbing a moribund Debenhams and then the 'challenged' Burton Group by the scruff of their necks and transforming the cultures and operating models to create two very profitable and sustainable businesses. Much of this was dependent on his wit, wisdom and extraordinary attention to detail. His insights and words of wisdom are well worth reading and reflecting upon and likely to help you create your recipes for success!'

Phil Wrigley, Chairman of Hobbs, Chairman of Majestic Wines, former Chairman of New Look

'It is intensely satisfying to read a book by someone who really knows what they're talking about – having "Been There, Done That" at the highest level. John Hoerner, who has been the Big Boss at most of Britain's important retailers, takes trouble to explain precisely how it's done, step by step, and the pitfalls to watch out for.

Anyone who reads this book will have a major advantage over their rivals in the race to the boardroom. It should be a mandatory set text on every business and retail marketing course.'

Nicholas Coleridge CBE, President, Condé Nast International

Comments from leading Chinese retail experts

'As soon as I started reading the manuscript, I finished the book without stopping . . . His use of the 'recipe' metaphor covers almost all aspects of retailing to be taken literally, as written, or used in combination with the reader's own ideas, experience and creativity.'

Mr Wenxin Zhu, CEO of SEC

'Mr John Hoerner is a senior retailer with more than 50 years' experience in the industry. The book explains profound things in a simple way . . . the retailers who read it may cook their own version of a retail feast.'

Mr Zhu Shiying (Dickson Chu), President of American Eagle Outfitters China

'This is a great, simple and effective book and it is presented logically and comprehensively . . . he really knows how to communicate simply with retail staff.'

Mr Steve Shen (Wenfeng Shen), CEO of Tommy Hilfiger China

'One idea in the book that I particularly agree with is: "The boss gets 150 per cent of the good news and only about 10 per cent of the bad news. React to the bad as a 'sample' . . ." I have been following this advice since reading it in the book and as a result have a deeper understanding of my business. This is a rare book on the retail industry . . . if you are an entrepreneur, a professional manager, or just work in retail, you can benefit from it.'

Mr Chunxia Fu, CEO of GSLY Co., Ltd

This book is dedicated to my wife Lea who has lived through it all with me. Also, to my dogs Chris, Scar, Smarty, Squeeze, Oscar, Scratch, Sniffy, Tyler, Angel, Tubby, Flower, Harley, Slate, Minnie and Charlie who have taught me so much about life. Lastly, to my many colleagues in 12 countries who have put up with me so generously over the years.

John Hoerner

To the reader:

I have written this book for everyone, from colleagues on the shop floor to chief executives. The style is simple. You will either get it or you won't very quickly. Most topics cover one or two pages. This is not a text book – let's call it a handbook instead!

A good retail business is exactly like a good recipe in cooking – you have to have all the ingredients in place. The better the quality of the ingredients the better the results are. The more talent the chef has to blend them together in the right quantities and at the right time, the better the outcome.

The people I know who are good cooks enjoy cooking – they enjoy the challenge and thrive on the fact that it is not always the same. They also know that sometimes when they think they have done exactly the same thing, the outcome is different! Good retailers are exactly the same. They thrive on the challenge of trying to get the mix and the timing exactly right.

Likewise the people I know who are the very best in the retail business are those who are having fun. Retailing can be soul-destroying at times because you never really get it exactly right (though you can always get it better) and sometimes you get it spectacularly wrong. When that happens, just like a chef with a ruined pie, you have to learn from the experience and get on with it for next time.

I hope you enjoy my 'recipes for retail'. I have included some cooking ones as well, just for fun. You will notice that my food recipes are not exact – in fact sometimes maddeningly inexact. Following these recipes requires you to use your imagination and blend in your own ideas and your own experience. This is exactly what you will have to do with my retail recipes too!

Good luck in cooking up a big success!

John Hoerner

Contents

Chapter 1

CUSTOMERS

They are the ones who decide if the chef has got it right!

When you get it right for customers, almost EVERYTHING ELSE works . . . when you don't get it right for customers, almost NOTHING else works!

There are around 1.4 billion people in the world who survive on the equivalent of $1.55 (£1) a day. If this many people were a country, it would be the largest in the world – larger than India or China.

What this means is that in the normal context of retailing, as we know it, customers don't really NEED anything that they buy from you.

They only buy what they think they need or want. This means emotion and personality enter into the transaction – both theirs and yours.

The second thing to remember is that not only do they not NEED anything they are buying from you, even if the WANT is strong, there are lots of other places they can get it.

There are also lots of competing priorities for discretionary income, not just what you are selling but what other people are selling as well.

A customer might trade off in their mind between new clothes and a holiday, or piano lessons for their children or a new laptop or iPhone.

Does someone who provides a nice restaurant compete with someone else who sells clothes? Definitely!

All of this adds up to the bottom line that all successful retailers start with people – how to make things great for people, which means the best products, the best prices, the best environment and the most confidence-building reputation.

That is what this recipe book is about . . . what it takes to cook up an irresistibly tasty dish for your customers.

All retailers **say** they listen to their customers. Most of them really **do** listen. Very few then really make a specific, well-planned and well-executed effort to **do something about it**.

One of the things I admired most when I first came to Tesco is the way they really did listen to customers. First they asked customers what THEY thought was important. They then asked customers to RATE Tesco on the things they thought were important.

Once this information was collected, Tesco developed specific programmes to deal with the issues that CUSTOMERS thought were important.

One specific example came about in 1994 when customers said: 'We don't like queuing!'

Tesco responded with a programme called 'one in front' and trained more members of staff in each store to operate the tills. They introduced systems for measuring the length of the queue so that, when required, all the tills could be opened. However, they did not stop there; they made 'one in front' a key measurement for the store manager's performance.

The customer would have no way of knowing this but every time a customer comes to the till the cashier enters a number that shows how many people are in the queue at the time. This becomes a permanent record by hour of the queue-management quality in that store.

I have never seen any other retailer, including the ones I have been in charge of, make such an impressive effort to do what their customers wanted.

And, to top it all, Tesco went back to the customers a year later and asked them to rate Tesco again on the key factors that Tesco had been working on. The exact amount of progress was therefore measurable.

'You can fool all the people some of the time and some of the people all of the time, but you cannot fool all the people all the time.'

US President Abraham Lincoln (attrib.)

I have learned over the years to have tremendous faith in what I call 'the collective intelligence of customers'.

Elsewhere in this book I will say, 'Your PR is not what you say you are; it is what you really are.'

Whatever you do with product, service, ethical trading, truth in advertising, keeping faith with your employees, your suppliers, and your customers, it will eventually be known and will become your brand and your reputation.

If you have a good reputation and you do something shady, you are 'selling off' some of your reputation. If you give your customers a little more than they expect, i.e. greater value, better quality or better service, then you are INVESTING in your reputation.

You will see in the next section that I do not have too much faith in the concept of what retailers call 'customer loyalty'.

Your customers – as a group – know what you are. To the extent that you keep the faith, they will keep coming to you because you are what you are.

Trying to fool customers with inferior product, misleading advertising or any other 'sharp' practice might give you a short-term benefit but in the long term you will be found out.

Building a good reputation takes effort, discipline and dedication by very good people over a long time. 'Selling it off' can be done overnight by almost anybody.

The best businesses always strive to invest in putting value into their 'reputation bank'. Countless businesses have fallen into the trap of 'selling off' their reputation and woken up with nothing left but memories of former glory.

'Customer Loyalty' is a myth. What does exist is 'familiarity' and 'habit'. As long as customers are satisfied, they keep coming. Let them down a few times and they are off like a shot to your competitors!

Dictionaries define loyalty as 'a feeling of allegiance' or 'an attitude of devoted attachment and affection'. This usually applies to friends or family.

I am always amazed at how the press and retailers bang on about 'customer loyalty' to retail stores or brands – I have yet to meet or see a 'loyal' customer.

The term 'loyalty' implies that the customer will keep coming **no matter what** – that is what loyalty means.

Actual customer behaviour is usually the opposite of this and what is **mistakenly** termed 'loyalty' is customers shopping in your store because of what they can get from you. They like shopping with you because they get what they want at the right price and at the right time and the service level is acceptable to them. They LIKE shopping there!

It does not take much in the way of bad experience to expose this so-called 'loyalty' for what it really is – the habit of shopping time and again with a retailer who treats you right and meets your needs.

What retailers call 'customer loyalty' has to be earned every day, in every way, with every transaction. Relying on people who are in the 'habit' of shopping with you without continuing to earn and deserve this so-called loyalty is a downhill road.

Customers vote with their money and their feet – every day. Treat them right and you will be re-elected every day.

You lose customers by the dozens – you gain them one at a time!
So:
Don't **kick** things out – customers, products or suppliers – 'squeeze' them out instead.

There is a mathematical reason for this.

Losing customers is usually about not having the product or service they want – this could be because you have discontinued it or because you are 'out of stock' – either way the customer cannot get from you what they were used to getting so they go elsewhere.

Another way of losing customers is poor service or poor handling of complaints. While people rarely talk about good service (because they expect it), they will tell everyone they know about a bad product or bad service experience. (Reverse 'viral' marketing!)

So, each customer that is lost because of service turns off several others. The customer lost by not having the product is joined by all the others who formerly bought that same product. The effect is instantaneous. Customers leave in groups.

On the other hand, gaining customers is a 'one at a time' proposition. They presumably were not starving or naked before you introduced your new line. This means it takes time for people to get used to you being a good place to shop.

This brings me to point two – if you eliminate a category, a product, a line or a supplier, you will lose that business instantly. You may not gain the replacement business instantly. Therefore, there is always a huge cost to 'major surgery'.

So, it is a much better idea to 'grow' the business that you feel is part of the future – put a lot of effort into it. Let the business that you feel is part of the past be 'squeezed out' by selling lots of the new good stuff. If you succumb to the temptation to kick it out, you might get a nasty surprise.

I remember a new CEO a few years ago in a chain of department stores who decided he did not like the 'budget floor' and closed it down forthwith. He lost all those budget customers overnight. It took three years to make up the lost sales and profit from this move and the same thing could have been achieved much more easily just by cutting it back over time and replacing it with the desired new product.

If your business is *failing*, you **might** need *revolution*; if your business is *successful*, *evolution* is much the better strategy.

Selling poor-quality, cheap products
to low-income
customers is an
immoral con.
Bad quality
is the worst
possible value.

It is a fallacy that people don't want, appreciate or deserve quality just because they have a limited budget. In some ways quality is even more important to customers with a limited income.

'Throw-away fashion' may be OK for a spoilt teenager on a generous budget but people who have to watch every penny need to have things that will last and last.

Don't fall into the trap of thinking that customers living on a limited budget want 'cheap' merchandise – what they need is products they can afford!

'If I had asked
customers what they
wanted, they would
have said a faster
horse!'

Henry Ford

'Don't give
customers what
they think they want;
give them what they
recognise as being
right when they
see it!'

Joseph Noble, Retail Consultant

Listening to customers is important, but customers also love new ideas. They can't know they want something that they've never seen before.

It is the job of the retailer to make sure they see what meets customers' needs today, not necessarily what sold last year.

The past can be a good indicator of the future but it is not the only indicator. This is one reason buyers have to use good suppliers and they also need to spend plenty of time outside their offices looking at other retailers and how customers live.

This is not only the job of the buyer; it is the job of the stores too. Displaying a new product so that customers will be sure to see it is important. Understanding a new product so it can be explained to customers is also important.

It might be true that 80 per cent to 90 per cent of what we sell is 'predictable' – but the 10 per cent to 20 per cent that is new, exciting and educational is what differentiates one retailer from another.

Chapter 2

STORES

This is the beautiful table where the retail 'dinner' is served to the customers.

Almost no one really <u>NEEDS</u> what they buy from your store – the trick is to make them want to buy!

BASIC PRINCIPLES:

1. When a customer looks at a department, if they cannot figure out what is going on in about five seconds, they probably won't bother.

2. Learn to look at your store like a customer – a 12-year-old customer – in a hurry – under a lot of pressure – and unfamiliar with your store. If your layout and visual passes this test, it is probably OK.

3. The only people who stand still looking at a department are people who work in the head office or the store. Customers are on the move all the time. Test your layout and visual by walking by quickly – not standing there 'studying' the department.

4. The store is a **theatre**. The layout of your department is the **stage**. The decor and visual merchandising are the **scenery**. The product is the **show**.

5. **Standards** are making sure everyone in the department knows what to do. **Discipline** is doing it all day, every day.

6. There are only two acceptable reasons for putting something in valuable space such as the window or the front of the department (see overleaf).

7. If a sign talks to the customer about product, it should be as close to that product as possible.

8. Use the space on the sign to tell the customer something they can't tell by just looking. 'Men's Jackets' on top of a rail of men's jackets is a waste of communication space. Tell them something about the product like 'Fully waterproof – breathable' jackets.

9. It is hard to do a **bad** job of presenting a great quantity of highly desirable merchandise complete in sizes and colours.

10. It is difficult to do a **good** job of presenting **assorted various items** in various styles, colours and sizes.

There are only two reasons to use prime space – either you know it sells and you are trying to sell more or you are testing to see if something new does sell.

Nothing else is worthwhile and in fact can be detrimental. See the chart below, which demonstrates the outcomes you get from different policies on how prime space is to be used:

Possible Use of Prime Space	Result for the Customer	**Result for your Business**
Sell more of something good that sells well.	Customer exposed to best product.	**Sell more of good styles and be attractive to customers.**
Trying to find out if something new is good or not.	Customer exposed to new product.	**Can find out quickly if new product worth repeating.**
Don't pay any attention to what goes in front.	Random effect depending on chance.	**Potential assets not utilised.**
Use prime space to try to 'push' something that is not selling.	Customer exposed to product that has already been rejected.	**Product does not sell anyway and customers are 'turned off'.**

No matter what you do, it does not matter if the customer cannot see it!

Product is number one – of course it is, along with staying in stock, and at the right price and at the right time – everyone knows that.

However, if the customer cannot see the product easily as they look at the department, they may never know what you have accomplished.

It has been proven over and over again that choice is only choice when the customer can see it.

Choice is also only choice when the styles really are different from each other. 'Me too' styles just add to confusion and make it harder for customers to see the really good ones.

Store decor must
be appropriate
for the nature of
the business . . .
good enough to
give confidence
but not so grand
as to intimidate or
negatively affect
price perception.

A few years ago we developed a new format for Evans –
the Burton Group large-size business. It cost no more than
the previous format and looked a lot better. We were really
pleased with how clever the store designers had been to
upgrade the look of the stores with no increase in budget. We
re-fitted four stores as a 'trial' of the new concept (always a
good idea).

We were shocked to see that the sales went down in every
store after the re-fit. We researched customer views and
learned that the customers felt that we had raised the prices.

In fact, the prices were identical to what they were before.
Customers also felt that the new store was 'maybe not for
them' or they had to 'be dressed properly before they came in'.

When I had this experience I remembered back to my father's
combined estate agent and property management business
60 years ago in Lincoln, Nebraska. The office area was
carpeted but the area where people came in to pay their rent
(in those days people paid weekly, often in cash) had a lino
floor.

The house sales staff constantly lobbied my dad to carpet the
front-desk area as well as they felt it did not look right.

Well, guess what, he finally gave in and carpeted the front and
the rent collections went down. He quickly realised that many
of the people who were renting were construction workers and
they stopped in on Friday to pay the rent after they had been
paid in cash. The new carpet made them feel that maybe they
should not come in with their work shoes on and once that
cash got away it was hard to come back the next week or send
their wife in to pay.

Store decor should be attractive, of course, but its main
purpose is to serve as a backdrop for the merchandise.

If you set out to 'impress' customers with your decor, I suggest
you should be in a pretty high-priced premium business. If
I had to make a rule that would work in 99 per cent of cases,
I would spend time, effort and money to 'impress' customers
with the product, and not with the store decor!

In a complex business it is hard to make display and layout 'rules' – principles are better, and there has to be a 'hierarchy of priorities': all principles are not equally important!

The following is what a list of floor-display principles – *in priority order* – might look like for your business:
(Some principles are more important and outrank the ones further down the list if you have to decide between them.)

1. There must be enough total fixtures in the department plan to support the sales plan based on the history of that store.

2. The mix between the departments, **including concessions** and within the departments, reflects both the **current** business and **potential** business for that store.

3. All categories are together. Squares are best. Rectangles are OK. Jigsaw puzzle piece shapes are not OK. (See diagrams on p. 29.)

4. Categories are clearly defined by aisles, walls, high gondolas and signage. (See the note at the end of the list.)

5. All categories are easy for the customer to identify and find as they walk through the store.

6. The customer can easily access all departments and products.

7. The adjacencies of the layout make sense to the customer. (See diagrams overleaf.)

8. Each category is well presented and is appealing to the customer.

9. Concessions and own-buy 'brands' have the identification they need for that brand.

10. Each category has appropriate display features.

11. Each category has a frontage on to either a primary aisle or a secondary visual aisle.

12. Visual aisles leading to a back wall have customer-attracting product displays at the end of the aisles.

13. Customers have visibility into or through the department.

Note: when making departments clear for customers, a good way to define the categories is through the use of space between fixtures.

If there is not a visual aisle between the departments, you can use fixture spacing, i.e. make the space BETWEEN THE CATEGORIES bigger than the space BETWEEN THE FIXTURES within a category.

Adjacency example:

Good	
Big Boys	**Big Girls**
Little Boys	**Little Girls**

Confusing	
Big Boys	**Big Girls**
Little Girls	**Little Boys**

Layout example:

Good	
Big Boys	**Big Girls**
Little Boys	**Little Girls**

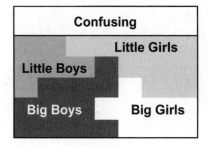

Customers are not mind readers and very few of them have the time or inclination to 'explore'.

Tell people clearly what you have for sale and how to get there.

This is particularly important in multi-level stores. It amazes me how so many retailers spend literally millions building stores and stocking them with lovely product only to totally fail when it comes to telling the customer what is upstairs.

The rule should be: if the customer cannot see it then they don't know it is there unless you tell them.

Outside the store or at the main entrance you should have a menu of what is available inside. Once again, at the bottom of each escalator or elevator you should have a menu of what is to come. The more attractive and legible these menus are, the better.

When it comes to identifying aisles of product, signs should be turned so they can be read from the main traffic aisle. Otherwise they are only of value once the customer is already there and can already see what is there.

The way to know if your wayfinding signs are any good or not is to pretend that you have never been in the store before, you are in a hurry and you have no particular interest in anything other than the one product you came in to buy.

How easy is it for you to find what you came in for?

How attractive and interesting is the store to make you want to visit other departments once you are in the store?

As in store visiting, the main problem with store design and vertical and horizontal wayfinding is that the people responsible for them know too much. They think about what they are doing and how wonderful it is rather than what it is like to be a customer in the store for the first time.

Most big retailers underestimate what a big factor store staff can be in their success.

Back in the days when retailing was a series of small, family-owned shops where the proprietor was on the scene all the time and in many cases had their family working in the shop, every transaction represented their livelihood. The high level of knowledge about the business and customer service was automatic.

Wind the clock forward to a chain with 50 or 100 or even 500 stores and think about what replaces this hands-on opportunity to connect with the customer.

Many executives, today, are running stores they have never seen and never will see. Some businesses spend millions on product, millions on advertising telling customers how wonderful they are, millions on building bigger and better and more stores, and then turn around and ignore the last connection to the customer – the staff in the store.

I am not just talking about having enough staff, which should be blindingly obvious to everyone, but about how the staff is informed about the product, the strategy of the business, the culture of the business and the commitment that the business makes to its customers.

Interaction between people – staff and customers – is never mechanical; it is about two human beings interacting with each other.

Therefore the attitude and the behaviour of the staff is as much a part of the 'brand' or the business as the products, the store itself, the marketing or the PR.

It is impossible to over-emphasise this!

It would be hard for me to imagine any programme that informed, involved and motivated store staff – whatever the cost – that would not pay off for your business. It might involve them attending an afternoon or a day workshop but the effect would be felt by hundreds of customers, day after day, throughout the year. The cost per customer contact would probably be in pennies!

In my first job at Hovland-Swanson (a single store) in Lincoln, Nebraska, I was a floor supervisor in the dress department. Each morning the dress buyer would hold a 'morning meeting' with the girls who worked in the department and show all the new product that came in and also ask for their feedback on what they had sold the previous day that people liked, etc. The meeting only lasted about 15 minutes. I noticed consistently that throughout the day I would hear the girls telling customers points of interest that the buyer had given in the morning meeting about product. It is possible, even in a big business, to replicate this type of contact but you have to be committed to it, work hard at it constantly, and invest time and money in it.

Having a well-trained, well-informed staff on the selling floor is a 'secret weapon'.

There are lots of other places where a customer can buy exactly what you sell.

It has always amazed me how many retailers invest **heavily** in time, money and effort in their sourcing of great product and then try to **skimp** on the last and most important link with the customer.

Saving money on store staff below optimum levels is 'stepping over a pound to pick up a penny'!

Note: 99% of retailers measure selling cost by % to sales. A much more valuable way is sales per hour worked – by day and time – this will result in the lowest cost!

Half of the information you get from store colleagues is of little value. The other half is invaluable. It is worth taking the time to listen to it all and sort out which is which.

My experience with British culture as opposed to American culture is that, in the UK, if you want information you have to ask for it.

I have found while touring stores for Debenhams, Burton Group, Arcadia and Tesco that colleagues are eager to share their views, IF ASKED. However, they will seldom volunteer information.

I made my store visits half pre-planned and half spontaneous. I also went half the time with colleagues from the head office and half the time on my own. All four permutations were valuable in their own special way in order to gain insight into store operation and what customers were saying and doing.

The important thing is to listen, and listen in a way that encourages people to talk to you. It rarely makes sense to have a negative conversation with a member of staff who is not in charge. If they knew what to do, they would be doing it.

Over the years I have picked up absolute jewels of ideas from colleagues who just gave me their views off the top of their heads because they are the ones who are there all day, every day, working with and listening to customers. This is because I asked and listened!

Tesco had a wonderful 'core value', which is 'Ask more than tell' – this is especially valuable when visiting stores. If you are running a lot of stores and you spend time 'telling', you might fix one thing in one store. If you spend time 'asking', you might get an idea that would help you fix 300 stores!

The number of retailers who really understand store lighting is almost none.

(And most of those work for Abercrombie or Hollister!)

UNDERSTANDING HOW THE HUMAN EYE WORKS

You cannot understand dramatic and effective store lighting if you don't understand how the human eye works. It is really a miraculous mechanism. Your eye can adapt to almost any light level. My son, who was in the US Marines at the time, proved to me that you can walk through a forest in the middle of the night just by the light of the stars. However, it takes two hours for your eyes to adjust fully and the glow from one cigarette would set you back 100 minutes!

It is all about contrast between light and shade. The more 'ambient' light you have, the more feature or 'spot' lighting you need to cut through it. The less ambient light, the less spot lighting is required. Abercrombie and Hollister have taken this to a level where there is NO ambient lighting AT ALL in their stores. Most retailers are not ready for this but they can still learn valuable lessons from it.

The best way to make the spot lighting effective is to reduce the ambient light. In many cases the 'spill' from the feature lighting is all you need to light the shop adequately for customers.

A good principle is that every bulb you burn (energy/cost) must be 'doing a job', i.e. pointing to product. I would be relentless about this. When you find a spotlight pointing to the floor or a blank wall, it is a MISTAKE and it needs to be corrected. Shine it on product or save the money!

It should go without saying that you don't want to light things from the back. Having a spotlight on the back of a display that lights the back, leaves the front in shade and shines into the customers' eyes as they view the display is another MISTAKE and needs to be corrected.

Very sadly, most retailers and retail architects and designers think about lighting their stores rather than lighting the PRODUCTS they are trying to sell. This is a huge blunder.

If I could go around again and have another career, I would like to be a retail lighting consultant – I think I could make a fortune.

Using concession specialists or brands can add to both your profitability and your customer appeal. The trick is to get the right ones for the right reasons.

Most large-space retailers and many small-space retailers have learned the advantages of sometimes using concessions to round out their customer offer.

The concessionaire has a defined space, is responsible for the staffing, and does all the inventory management and stocking. They are also responsible for any stock loss. They pay an agreed percentage to the store owner on the sales that they make, which are usually run through the store owner's till along with their own-buy sales.

Good concessions are transparent to the customer. They only see something they like and are able to buy it. In a perfect world, there should be no difference between a customer buying from a concession and from an owned department. (In the real world, unfortunately, concessions usually give better sales assistance!)

The trick is to manage concessions as diligently as you do your own business. This means periodic reviews and updates on stock content and how the business is performing.

The best measure of how a concession is contributing is income per square metre (or square foot), which can be compared to the same statistic for other concessions and owned departments.

Store managers should be just as interested in how their concession departments are doing as they are in the owned departments.

With online selling growing dramatically in most countries, space in big stores will become more available. Concessions can be an excellent solution to efficient space use.

'YCDBSOYA'

('You Can't Do Business Sitting On Your Arse!')

The founder of Tesco, Jack Cohen, used to have a tie clasp that said 'YCDBSOYA'. Most people assumed it was some obscure Yiddish word but all his store managers knew what it was and that it stood for 'You can't do business sitting on your arse'.

When I became Chairman and Chief Executive of Debenhams in 1987 the store managers were called 'Store Directors' and had lavish offices – some with fireplaces! This was a throwback to the old days when the parts of Debenhams were individual, privately owned local department stores. The Store Directors loved spending time in their offices and summoning their minions for 'conferences'.

One of my first actions – unpopular with the people involved but loved by almost everyone else (including the customers) – was to abolish the title of 'Store Director' and substitute 'Store Manager'.

We made a new policy that the office time had to be limited to only the work that HAD to be done in the offices. The manager's real job was out on the floor talking to customers and staff and seeing what was going on.

In 1992, when I became head of the Burton Group with over 2,000 shops, we made an even stiffer rule for small shops and actually eliminated the managers' offices – a symbolic move but an important statement about where the job physically should be.

Think about all the world's best and most famous restaurants – they are usually run by an owner who is on the scene, out in front or in the kitchen, making sure that everything is as it should be for customers.

Just today, before writing this page, I had Sunday lunch at Nolita in Shanghai. The place was JAMMED with customers. Happy customers! Both the owner and his wife were on the floor to make sure everything was working perfectly both in the kitchen and serving customers at the tables.

One of the often disappointing aspects of patronising national and international chains is that, due to a series of little things that do not happen or do not happen properly, it appears that the service is given (or, more accurately, not given) by people who just don't care!

One way of ensuring that the sales team cares is to make sure that the top person (i.e. the store manager) demonstrates all day, every day, that they care . . . and you cannot do that sitting in an office!

Most of the benefit of re-fitting a store comes from re-mixing the business – not from the cosmetic appearance.

I learned quickly when renovating Debenhams stores that there was a huge benefit in 're-mixing' the business at the time of the re-fit.

Departments that have too much space invariably have too much stock and this causes high markdowns. Departments that have too little space fail to optimise their potential.

When you have the opportunity to re-fit a store or build a new store, one of the biggest mistakes you can make is to get hung up on the 'appearance' and neglect the fundamentals of space allocation.

On the opposite page is the type of analysis you should be doing anyway. This serves as the basis to optimise the use of space. The store will look just as good or better and you will have allocated a precious asset intelligently.

Information Required to Assess and Analyse Store Performance

Excel spreadsheet with columns as follows:

| F I | = needs to be filled in |
| CAL | = spreadsheet should calculate |

Column number:		Information contained:
1	F I	Name of store
2	F I	Last year annual sales (this and all following columns sub-totalled by region and total)
3	F I	Square metres of space dedicated to department
4	CAL	Sales per square metre (as appropriate to your planning system)
5	CAL	Sales per square foot (as appropriate to your planning system)
6	F I	Margin cash (if you don't have cash and you know per cent, these two rows can be reversed and you can enter percent and calculate cash)
7	CAL	Margin per cent
8	CAL	Margin cash per square metre
9	CAL	Margin cash per square foot
10	F I	Number of 'mods' (define a mod and mod equivalent)
11	CAL	Sales per mod
12	CAL	Margin per mod
13	F I	Linear feet/metres of hang space (or equivalent)
14	CAL	Sales per linear foot/metre
15	CAL	Margin per linear foot/metre
16	F I	Sales participation to total non-food or food (if your business is both food and general merchandise)
17	F I	Sales participation to total store

NB A 'mod' is whatever your business uses for planning purposes to describe a unit of display area – it has to be the same throughout the store

Once you have this information you can set about 're-mixing'
the business – this should include not only the business you
are doing now but the business you envision for the future as
this store re-fit will probably have to last five years or more and
changing around departments is expensive.

As a personal policy, I would never look at any store layout
plan without at the same time having someone show me the
plans to re-mix the space to the optimum.

The following table is complex and the numbers are for
illustration only but it shows how you can re-mix a business
and improve the profitability and sales with the product mix
remaining just as it is now.

My argument would be that the profit density will end up being
better than this because the departments with too much space
will improve their margin performance by having to carry less
stock which ends up being marked down.

The departments with potential can transform their ranges by
being given enough space.

It would take a book bigger than this one entirely devoted to
the subject to cover it thoroughly but the principle is what is
important.

Make sure you have a well-thought-out 'As Is' and 'To Be'
financial plan for space before you start drawing plans!

EXAMPLE – RE-MIXING THE SPACE ALLOCATED IMPROVES PROFITS WITH ALL OTHER FACTORS REMAINING THE SAME:

	Metres²			Sales Density			Sales			Profit Density			Profit		
	Current	Opt	Var	Current	Opt	Var	Current	Opt	Var	Current	Opt	Var	Current	Opt	Var
Bed and Bath	55	90	64%	£93.2	£85.4	-8%	£5,127	£7,689	50%	£36.2	£32.5	-10%	£1,993	£2,923	47%
Books	30	45	50%	£77.2	£75.9	-2%	£2,315	£3,418	48%	£19.6	£19.6	0%	£587	£881	50%
Car Care	15	30	100%	£119.9	£104.3	-13%	£1,798	£3,128	74%	£56.4	£46.2	-18%	£847	£1,385	64%
Cards & Party	60	100	67%	£136.6	£108.8	-20%	£8,197	£10,878	33%	£78.2	£61.7	-21%	£4,690	£6,171	32%
Cook & Dine	105	110	5%	£86.3	£84.0	-3%	£9,058	£9,245	2%	£37.8	£36.8	-3%	£3,965	£4,043	2%
Digital Cameras	10	20	100%	£211.5	£188.1	-11%	£2,115	£3,761	78%	£27.3	£24.6	-10%	£273	£492	80%
DIY & Paint	55	20	-64%	£49.1	£115.2	135%	£2,699	£2,304	-15%	£13.0	£39.0	199%	£716	£779	9%
Domestic Electrical	80	80	0%	£95.9	£95.9	0%	£7,672	£7,672	0%	£24.7	£24.7	0%	£1,978	£1,978	0%
Electrical	85	150	76%	£241.9	£242.5	0%	£20,557	£36,377	77%	£41.5	£37.5	-10%	£3,532	£5,627	59%
Home Ents	150	95	-37%	£138.9	£210.4	51%	£20,835	£19,991	-4%	£12.1	£17.8	47%	£1,821	£1,691	-7%
Home Living	80	65	-19%	£50.9	£56.5	11%	£4,069	£3,670	-10%	£21.1	£24.1	14%	£1,687	£1,567	-7%
Home Office	95	95	0%	£113.4	£113.4	0%	£10,774	£10,774	0%	£38.1	£38.1	0%	£3,618	£3,618	0%
Home Utility	80	100	25%	£87.9	£81.5	-7%	£7,031	£8,154	16%	£39.9	£36.4	-9%	£3,193	£3,643	14%
Household	5	15	200%	£79.0	£63.3	-20%	£395	£950	141%	£36.0	£28.0	-22%	£180	£421	134%
Photo Albums	15	10	-33%	£25.1	£30.6	22%	£376	£306	-19%	£13.8	£16.9	22%	£208	£169	-19%
Sports and Leisure	95	75	-21%	£66.4	£77.1	16%	£6,311	£5,782	-8%	£24.5	£28.6	17%	£2,327	£2,146	-8%
Telecoms	35	0	-100%	£132.4	£0.0	-100%	£4,634	£0	-100%	£8.4	£0.0	-100%	£294	£0	-100%
Toys	110	90	-18%	£88.4	£94.5	7%	£9,721	£8,506	-13%	£17.7	£19.3	9%	£1,942	£1,738	-10%
Women's Wear	395	415	5%	£93.3	£91.2	-2%	£36,841	£37,832	3%	£37.2	£36.1	-3%	£14,685	£15,000	2%
Men's Wear	220	145	-34%	£61.5	£95.8	56%	£13,536	£13,888	3%	£20.6	£32.4	58%	£4,522	£4,698	4%
Kids' Wear	300	325	8%	£70.0	£67.6	-3%	£21,014	£21,983	5%	£32.1	£30.9	-4%	£9,643	£10,035	4%
TOTAL	2075	2075	0%	£94.0	£104.2	11%	£1,95,074	£2,16,309	11%	£30.2	£33.3	10%	£62,700	£69,003	10%

Opt = Optimum

Var = Variance to current

The growth of online shopping is astronomical – what will the effect be on traditional retail stores?

Every retailer is right to study and understand all the ramifications of increased internet shopping – not only from home and office computers but now from smartphones as well.

It is already possible to shop using a watch – who knows what electronic shopping method will be invented next?

However, the one thing the internet will never be able to do is allow you to touch, feel and examine the product and really compare it alongside similar products.

The second thing that is harder on the internet is to get a real person to discuss the pros and cons of the products you are looking at or help you find a product you are looking for.

Therefore, what seems obvious to me but may not be obvious to all retailers is that the way to make sure your 'bricks and mortar' store continues to prosper is to emphasise the things that this store can do that an online store cannot.

You will never stop or even slow down online shopping but what you can do is provide a viable alternative.

Also, most modern retailers are online as well as in stores so the better your stores look and the better your staff in the stores are at helping customers, the better your brand ranks in the minds of customers and the more trusted you will be on the internet.

It is a huge mistake for any retailer to treat online customers as somehow 'different' from in-store customers – they are all just customers looking to use their money in the most efficient and enjoyable way to increase their quality of life.

And finally . . .

The only acceptable excuse for dirt of any kind in a retail store is potting soil for live plants!

Chapter 3

BUYERS, SUPPLIERS & STOCK MANAGEMENT

These are the chefs who source and prepare the repast for the customers.

The most valuable thing you can teach your commercial team is how to think like a customer. Most buyers think about what they are **doing**, not what is **getting done** for the customer!

Thinking like a customer is dead easy if you know how to do it.

You have to put yourself into a kind of trance. Forget who you are and what you do. Forget what you know. Pretend for that moment that:

1. You have never been in the store before.
2. You are in a huge hurry. (I always try to imagine a mother with a young child who is desperate for the loo!)
3. You came in for another reason entirely.
4. Then, if possible (and I know this is really hard for you), try to pretend that you don't know anything at all about stores or retailing!

Then look at your department:

☐ How attractive is it?
☐ What would make you want to come in at all?
☐ How easy would it be for you to shop and find something?
☐ What product messages are you getting?

I use this to test departments and also wayfinding signs in the store.

The reason most retailers don't get enough out of their store visits is that they know too much. When you clear your brain of what you know or think you know and start **seeing what an ordinary shopper in a hurry sees**, you will look at your department or store a lot differently.

Good buyers know all about product. Good merchandise planners and finance executives know all about figures. Great retailers are equally at home with both.

When a pilot is landing an airplane there are two critical factors that must be monitored constantly. The first is the speed of the aircraft: too fast and you will overshoot the runway; too slow and you will fall out of the sky. There is only a small margin between these two, so you have to watch the speed constantly.

Also, at the same time, you have to be lined up with the runway – even a degree or two off makes a difference.

Therefore the pilot has to constantly look back and forth – check speed, check runway; check speed, check runway; constantly until the landing is complete.

It is the same with product and figures. You have to understand the product and what makes it sell, or not. However, you also have to constantly look at the figures to see what they tell you.

One is not more important than the other – they are both important and they both have to be looked at all the time, at the same time.

If you are a good buyer and want to be great, learn to understand and analyse figures!

If you are a good merchandise planner and want to be great, learn to understand and appreciate product!

Poor buyers don't plan.

Average buyers plan carefully what they are going to buy.

Good buyers plan carefully what they're going to sell, when and at what price, and then buy what is necessary to support the sales plan.

Great buyers add in sales promotion plans, visual presentation and sales associate training, and negotiate to ensure the profitability.

Genius buyers do all of the above except they start with what they want to achieve in the store and work backwards.
Which are you?

Three simple questions guaranteed to make you a great merchant and also a great teacher:

1. What are you going to do if the product sells better than you planned?

2. What are you going to do if it does not sell as well as you planned?

3. How did you figure that out?

Liquidity is the lifeblood of successful buying.

A buyer must always be in a position to buy.

Being hungry for new things is essential for the correct attitude in the marketplace.

If you doubt this statement, think back over the best buys you have ever made – were they offered to you or did you go after them?

When was the last time you saw a customer come into your shop and heard them ask, 'What's old?'

The fashion business thrives on newness. The stock you have purchased, no matter how much you are in love with it, is not fine wine – it does not improve with age!

Each department should have a plan to liquidate 95 per cent of all the stock by the end of the season. If you fail in this and end up carrying over this stock to a future season, it will not only affect your profitability but your future business.

However much you save by 'not taking' markdowns this season, it will cost you 50 per cent more or 100 per cent more when you do get around to taking them. This is like borrowing from a loan shark!

There is an added pitfall in carrying old stock. You continually expose your customers to things they have already seen and rejected. This tends to make you boring and sluggish compared to shops where the stock is moving all the time.

The absolute worst error you can make is allocating good floor space to old rejected product in the hope that you can somehow make it into something good. (see page 21.)

Floor space is wasted on BAD OLD PRODUCT at the wrong prices because:

1. It does not work.
2. It exposes the worst of what you have to customers.

Clothing goes off over time just like cheese or fruit. It just takes a little longer. The customers still know that it stinks, even if you don't!

When you are
overstocked and
buyers are in
defensive mode,
it brings out the
worst of all worlds.

A heavy stock is
always incomplete!

If you have the right discipline in your business, then buyers will be required to 'pull in their horns' when stocks are heavy. The ramifications of this are far-reaching.

For one thing, if you have a proper 'open-to-buy' process, the open-to-buy will be curtailed.

If a buyer is overstocked, they will be in defensive mode – trying to get rid of what they already have.

This makes them less open to new ideas, good deals from suppliers, filling in on needed items and repeating orders on good items. Generally, they take up a whole raft of 'business-limiting' stances.

In my experience good buyers are 'hungry buyers' – they are always on the lookout for a good deal or a new idea on behalf of their customers.

When you are spending sleepless nights trying to concoct ways of digesting product that does not sell or getting your stocks down, you are not aggressively in the marketplace seeking out new ideas and good deals on behalf of your customers.

By mathematical definition, the more stock you have in relation to your sales, the higher the proportion of the stock that consists of things the customer has already rejected or does not want.

Therefore, a lean stock with a hungry buyer is more likely to contain things people want than a fat stock with a buyer bunkered up trying to solve problems instead of exploiting opportunities.

You can take my word for this or you can plough through all the spreadsheets that prove the point in the examples later in this chapter.

'Trialling' or 'testing' is only effective if you set it up right – there has to be statistical validity to the trial!

I cannot imagine the number of times a buyer has said to me, we are going to trial this in our best stores. This is not a trial – this is a buy for the best stores.

There is nothing wrong with that but don't call it a 'trial'.

If you really want to find out whether something is good or not, buy it for an array of stores that mirrors your entire estate of stores – large, medium and small, affluent and not so affluent, and heavy competition and not so heavy competition.

When you analyse that performance, you will then have an idea of how well the idea would have performed across all your stores.

One other mistake to avoid is to have 'test stores' – this also creates a distortion.

You should have several arrays of 'test pattern' stores that you can use in rotation to test new product ideas. This testing will give more stores new ideas and excitement and will also spread the risk of testing across all the stores.

Some of the most risky merchandise you buy can also be some of the most exciting. That way by testing with a statistical set of stores you keep excitement in many more stores and your tests really are valid.

Another rule I have is **'Don't re-test!'**

This means set it up right (as above) and then, if the test is good, have the courage to buy the product for all the stores or all the stores in which you think it will work. The idea of testing and then re-testing means that your bottom stores will rarely get anything new or exciting and by the time they do the customers will probably have moved on to something else – this will then reinforce your view that they are bad stores!

Sourcing from good factories with safe premises and good working conditions is not just taking the moral high ground – it is good business.

- All the products you sell should be safe, legal, of good quality and sustainably sourced regardless of where or how they are sold.
- Work with suppliers who operate good, safe and clean factory standards, who control their raw materials and processes, and who treat all the workers in their supply chain fairly. Check on this regularly to be sure that standards are being met and that suppliers source their raw materials with the same integrity with which they operate their sites.
- It is a good idea to hold detailed product specifications for all the lines you sell and regularly check to ensure customers are getting what you specified.
- Some retailers may be tempted to think that sourcing from dodgy factories with low-paid workers or secondary working conditions is a clever way to save money or make a higher margin. My experience has been the opposite. You always get a better deal and better product from suppliers who operate ethically.
- Suppliers who cut legal corners, safety corners and quality corners, and treat their own staff poorly, are the ones who will let you down and in turn let your customers down in the end – one way or another.

Good product does not come out of bad factories!

HOW TO DEAL WITH SUPPLIERS THE OUTDATED WAY:

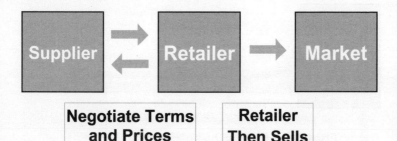

| Supplier ⇄ Retailer → Market |

Negotiate Terms and Prices   **Retailer Then Sells**

- A zero-sum game – buyer negotiates to get the best price, supplier negotiates to get the best price.
- They agree on a price, and then the buyer tries to sell it the best they can for the best margin.

(This old-fashioned approach assumes that the biggest opportunity is for the buyer to get some of the supplier's money or for the supplier to get some of the buyer's money.)

- The problem is that this approach completely ignores the big opportunity, which is for them to work together to get more revenue from the marketplace.
- Possibilities are limited to small advantages one might gain from the other.
- The relationship is adversarial, not trusting.
- This involves suspicion that you might not be getting the best deal.

HOW TO DEAL WITH SUPPLIERS THE MODERN, RIGHT WAY:

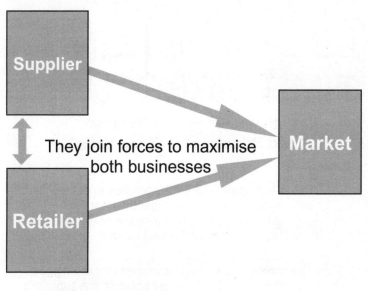

- Unlimited opportunity.
- A partnership relationship.
- Builds trust.
- Open and transparent.
- Taps the market potential by making customers happy.
- Complete opposite of a 'zero-sum' game.
- Incentivises the supplier to support the retailer.

MONEY IS MONEY BUT TIME IS ALSO MONEY. LOSING SELLING TIME DIRECTLY AFFECTS SELL-THROUGH, WHICH DIRECTLY AFFECTS PROFIT.

Everyone knows that fresh produce has a limited shelf-life and a sell-by date. It is therefore obvious that any time in the supply chain is time off the valuable selling time.

What a lot of people don't realise is that this same principle applies in other categories – clothing being a good example.

With rapidly changing fashion and seasonality, the majority of clothing products have a specific selling period and therefore late delivery directly affects the profit.

To explain this we make some assumptions. Have a look at the following two examples that demonstrate the way a clothing product might sell through in the business.

The realised margin is dependent on the sell-through.

Now imagine that for some reason the product is delayed by one week, while everything else remains the same.

In this case, if the sales for Week 4 are removed because the product is late, the following things happen:

- The sales go down by the sales for that week.
- The stock that did not sell then drops down and goes into the clearance process, which means reduced margin or a loss.
- So instead of selling this lost week's sales at a profit, you sell this amount of stock at a loss.
- You then get a 'balance-scales' effect where the profitable sales loss *reduces* the revenue and the liquidation of stock bought for sales that were lost *increases* the cost of markdowns.
- Losing even one week in clothing can affect the net margin at the end of the season by 5 or more percentage points and 20 per cent plus in cash margin.
- If you choose not to take my word for this, look at the following examples.
- If you don't like my numbers, plug in your own margin numbers and projected sales and work the maths out for your own operation.
- I guarantee you will be shocked at what just one lost week will cost you!

Typical Clothing Selling Cycle   **Example 1: Selling 60% of stock purchased at full price before clearance starts**

Profitability in clothing depends on % of sales at regular price plus timely and acceptable clearance patterns. With seasonal and/or fashion merchandise, there is always a 'cut-off' date for regular-price sales and a 'terminal' date for ending stock. (Any delay at outset shortens selling life with a big effect on margin.)

Selling Week	Price	Mark-downs £	Sales £	Sales £ Cum	% Orig Stock	% Stk Sold Cum	Remain Stock £	% Sold of Beg Stk	Wks OH Cover	Comment
At Start			0.0				100.0			
1	Reg. Pr.		6.0	6.0	6.0%	6.0%	94.0	6.0%	16.7	First week is usually 'partial'
2	Reg. Pr.		13.5	19.5	13.5%	19.5%	80.5	14.4%	7.0	First full week of sell
3	Reg. Pr.		10.5	30.0	10.5%	30.0%	70.0	13.0%	7.7	
4	Reg. Pr.		7.5	37.5	7.5%	37.5%	62.5	10.7%	9.3	
5	Reg. Pr.		6.5	44.0	6.5%	44.0%	56.0	10.4%	9.6	
6	Reg. Pr.		5.0	49.0	5.0%	49.0%	51.0	8.9%	11.2	
7	Reg. Pr.		4.5	53.5	4.5%	53.5%	46.5	8.8%	11.3	
8	Reg. Pr.		3.5	57.0	3.5%	57.0%	43.0	7.5%	13.3	
9	Reg. Pr.		3.0	60.0	3.0%	60.0%	40.0	7.0%	14.3	
		13.3	60.0		13.30%		26.7			First Clearance, 1/3 off
10	Third off		4.5	64.5	4.5%	64.5%	22.2	11.3%	5.9	
11	Third off		3.0	67.5	3.0%	67.5%	19.2	13.5%	7.4	
12	Third off		2.0	69.5	2.0%	69.5%	17.2	10.4%	9.6	
		4.3	9.5		3.70%		12.9			Second Markdown, 50% off
13	Half Pr.		3.0	72.5	3.0%	72.5%	9.9	17.5%	4.3	
14	Half Pr.		1.5	74.0	1.5%	74.0%	8.4	15.2%	6.6	
		4.2	4.5		3.3%		4.2			Final Clearance, 75% off
15	75% off	21.8	2.0	76.0	2.0%	76.0%	2.2	23.9%	4.2	

Residue stock of 2.2 in cash represents 2.2% of purchase but residue stock is at 75% off, so at the original price it represents 8.8% of the original stock bought.

Regular price sales	£60.0
1/3 off sales	£9.5
1/2 price sales	£4.5
75% off sales	£2.0
Total Sales	£76.0

Sold	£76.00
Mkd Down	£21.80
Residue	£2.20
	£100.00

Clothing Margin Projection Based upon Selling Cycle

In this example 60% of stock is sold at regular price before clearance activity starts

Intake Margin:	50.0%
Stock Purchased:	£100.0
Sterling Intake Margin:	£50.0

Retail Price of Stock	% of Sales	% of Stock	Sales	Mark-down	MKD % to Sales	
						Sales are affected by quality, price, fashion appropriateness of the stock but also by whether or not it has the time to sell and is in the right quantity to be digested by the available potential business. Too much good stock becomes bad stock. Stock without time to sell becomes poorly-performing stock.
Sold at Reg. Price	78.9%	60.0%	£60.0	£0.0	0.0%	The better the original stock is, and the more
Sold at 1/3 off	12.5%	9.5%	£9.5	£13.3	140.3%	that sells at regular price, chances are that it will also move at the first markdown. If the stock
Sold at 1/2 price	5.9%	4.5%	£4.5	£4.3	95.4%	is not so good, or does not have time to sell,
Sold at 75% off	2.6%	2.0%	£2.0	£4.2	209.4%	then there is more chance it will take a second markdown
Total	100.0%	76.0%	£76.0	£21.8	28.7%	(or more) to clear.

Margin Calculation:

Cost of Goods:	£50.0		Stock Sold	£76.00
Retail Sales:	£76.0		Mkd Down	£21.80
Realised Margin:	£26.0		Residue	£2.20
Margin % to Sales:	34.2%			£100.00

Realised margin £ as a per cent to intake margin: **52.0%**

Future liability: £2.20 of stock to be cleared

Clothing Selling Cycle

Example 2: One week of regular-price selling lost due to late delivery to stores

Profitability in clothing depends on % of sales at regular price plus timely and acceptable clearance patterns. With seasonal and/or fashion merchandise, there is always a 'cut-off' date for regular-price sales and a 'terminal' date for ending stock. (Any delay at outset shortens selling life with effect on margin.)

Selling Week	Price	Mark-downs	Sales £	Sales £ Cum	Orig Stock	Stk Sold Cum	Remain Stock	Sold of Beg Stk	Wks OH Cover	Comment
Open			0.0				100.0			
1	Reg. Pr.		6.0	6.0	6.0%	6.0%	94.0	6.0%	16.7	First week is usually 'partial'
2	Reg. Pr.		13.5	19.5	13.5%	19.5%	80.5	14.4%	7.0	First full week of sell
3	Reg. Pr.		10.5	30.0	10.5%	30.0%	70.0	13.0%	7.7	
4	Reg. Pr.		0.0	30.0	0.0%	30.0%	70.0	0.0%	N/A	One week of RP sales missing
5	Reg. Pr.		6.5	36.5	6.5%	36.5%	63.5	9.3%	10.8	
6	Reg. Pr.		5.0	41.5	5.0%	41.5%	58.5	7.9%	12.7	
7	Reg. Pr.		4.5	46.0	4.5%	46.0%	54.0	7.7%	13.0	
8	Reg. Pr.		3.5	49.5	3.5%	49.5%	50.5	6.5%	15.4	
9	Reg. Pr.		3.0	52.5	3.0%	52.5%	47.5	5.9%	16.8	
		15.8			13.30%		31.7			First Clearance, 1/3 off
10	Third off		5.0	57.5	5.0%	57.5%	26.7	10.5%	6.3	
11	Third off		3.5	61.0	3.5%	61.0%	23.2	13.1%	7.6	
12	Third off		2.2	63.2	2.2%	63.2%	21.0	9.5%	10.5	
		5.2			3.70%		15.7			Second Markdown, 50% off
13	Half Pr.		3.3	66.5	3.3%	66.5%	12.4	15.7%	4.8	
14	Half Pr.		1.5	68.0	1.5%	68.0%	10.9	12.1%	8.3	
		5.5			3.3%		5.5			Final Clearance, 75% off
15	75% off	26.5	2.1	70.1	2.1%	70.1%	3.4	19.2%	5.2	

Residue stock of 3.4 in cash represents 3.4% of purchase but residue stock is at 75% off, so at the original price it represents 13.6% of the original stock bought. This compares to residue of 2.2 or 8.8% at original price in the previous example.

Regular-price sales	£52.5
1/3 off sales	£10.7
1/2 price sales	£4.8
75% off sales	£2.1
	£70.1

Sold	£70.10
Mkd Down	£26.50
Residue	£3.40
	£100.00

Cum = Cumulative

Clothing Margin Projection Based upon Selling Cycle

In this example only 52.5% of stock is sold at regular price before clearance due to the lost week of regular-price selling

Intake Margin:	50.0%
Stock Purchased:	£100.0
Sterling Intake Margin:	£50.0

Retail Price of Stock	% of Sales	% of Stock	Sales	Mark-down	MKD % to Sales
Sold at Reg. Price	74.9%	52.5%	£52.5	£0.0	0.0%
Sold at 1/3 off	15.3%	10.7%	£10.7	£15.8	148.0%
Sold at 1/2 price	6.8%	4.8%	£4.8	£5.2	109.2%
Sold at 75% off	3.0%	2.1%	£2.1	£5.5	260.1%
Total	100.0%	70.1%	£70.1	£26.5	37.9%

Margin Calculation:

Cost of Goods:	£50.0
Retail Sales:	£70.1
Realised Margin:	£20.1
Margin % to Sales:	28.7%

Sold	£70.10
Mkd Down	£26.50
Residue	£3.40
	£100.00

Realised Margin as a per cent to intake margin: **40.2%**

Sales lost compared to Example 1: £76.0 - £70.1 = £5.9 - 7.8%

£ Margin lost compared to Example 1 is £26.0 - £20.1 or £5.9
22.6% of margin in Example 1 lost by the one-week delay!
Plus you have 1.4 more in residue stock to liquidate in the future.

Sales are affected by quality, price, fashion appropriateness of the stock but also by whether or not it has the time to sell and is in the right quantity to be digested by the available potential business. Too much good stock becomes bad stock.

Stock without time to sell becomes poorly performing stock. In this case a week of regular-price selling has been lost!

The better the original stock is, and the more that sells at regular price, chances are that it will also move at the first markdown. If the stock is not so good, or does not have time to sell, then there is more chance it will take a second markdown (or more) to clear.

Stock-turn equals profit. The faster your stock turns, the more money you make. The only valid reason to have stock around is to support the sales level.

Stock Cover Summary:

21 weeks' cover means 147 days of stock on hand.
   This means for everything sold that day – customer
   has 147 things to choose from.

14 weeks' cover means 98 days of stock on hand.
   This means for everything sold that day – customer
   has 98 things to choose from.

7 weeks' cover means 49 days of stock on hand.
   This means for everything sold that day – customer
   has 49 things to choose from.

Heavy stocks are always incomplete due to pressure on
open-to-buy.

Heavy stocks make it hard for customer to buy as there is too
much to choose from – confusion rather than choice.

Using the BEST POSSIBLE CASE – which is FIFO – i.e. 'First
In First Out'.

If you run 21 weeks stock, things have to wait 147 days for
their turn to sell – this is almost 5 months.

If you run 14 weeks stock, things have to wait 98 days for their
chance to sell – this is over 3 months.

If you run 7 weeks stock, things have to wait 49 days for their
chance to sell – this is a month and a half.

Of course stock does not sell in 'turn' – the good things sell
faster and the new things will sell faster, which means the old
things get older.

Once stock gets old, it costs more to liquidate.

   The cost of clearing goods in season is usually 45%
   of the original value.
   The cost of clearing goods one year old is usually
   75% of the value.
   The cost of clearing goods over one year old is
   usually 90% of the value.

Analysis of why running with too much stock causes higher markdowns and lost sales

7 Weeks' Cover Profile Week:	1	2	3	4	5	6	7	8	9	10	11	12	13	14	15	Season total:
BOW Total Stock	70	70	70	70	70	70	70	70	70	70	70	70	70	70	70	
Previous Season Stock	10	8	6	5	4	4	4	4	4	4	4	4	4	4	3	
This Season Stock	60	62	64	65	66	66	66	60	50	41	33	26	19	12	6	
Next Season Stock	0	0	0	0	0	0	0	0	16	25	33	40	47	54	61	
check	70	70	70	70	70	70	70	70	70	70	70	70	70	70	70	
Week Total Intake	10	10	10	10	10	10	10	10	10	10	10	10	10	10	10	
Previous Season Intake	0	0	0	0	0	0	0	0	0	0	0	0	0	0	0	
This Season Intake	10	10	10	10	10	10	4	10	0	0	0	0	0	0	0	
Next Season Intake	0	0	0	0	0	0	6	0	10	10	10	10	10	10	10	
check	10	10	10	10	10	10	10	10	10	10	10	10	10	10	10	
Week Total Sales	10	10	10	10	10	10	10	10	10	10	10	10	10	10	10	150.00
Previous Season Sales	2	2	1	1	0	0	0	0	0	0	0	0	0	1	1	
This Season Sales	8	8	9	9	10	10	10	10	9	8	7	7	7	6	5	
Next Season Sales	0	0	0	0	0	0	0	0	1	2	3	3	3	3	4	
check	10	10	10	10	10	10	10	10	10	10	10	10	10	10	10	
Total Cover	7	7	7	7	7	7	7	7	7	7	7	7	7	7	7	
Previous Season Cover	5.0	4.0	6.0	5.0												
This Season Cover	7.5	7.8	7.1	7.2	6.6	6.6	6.6	6.0	5.6	5.1	4.7	3.7	2.7	2.0	1.2	
Next Season Cover									16.0	12.5	11.0	13.3	15.7	18.0	15.3	
Margin Per Cent	40.00%	40.00%	44.00%	43.00%	50.00%	50.00%	50.00%	50.00%	45.50%	46.00%	43.00%	43.00%	39.50%	33.00%	32.50%	43.30%
Previous Season Stock	0.00%	0.00%	-10.00%	-20.00%												
This Season Stock	50.00%	50.00%	50.00%	50.00%	50.00%	50.00%	50.00%	50.00%	45.00%	45.00%	40.00%	40.00%	35.00%	30.00%	25.00%	
Next Season Stock	50.00%	50.00%	50.00%	50.00%	50.00%	50.00%	50.00%	50.00%	50.00%	50.00%	50.00%	50.00%	50.00%	50.00%	50.00%	
Margin Quantum	4.0	4.0	4.4	4.3	5.0	5.0	5.0	5.0	4.6	4.6	4.3	4.3	4.0	3.3	3.3	64.95
Previous Season Stock	0.0	0.0	-0.1	-0.2	0.0	0.0	0.0	0.0	0.0	0.0	0.0	0.0	0.0	0.0	0.0	
This Season Stock	4.0	4.0	4.5	4.5	5.0	5.0	5.0	5.0	4.1	3.6	2.8	2.8	2.5	1.8	1.3	
Next Season Stock	0.0	0.0	0.0	0.0	0.0	0.0	0.0	0.0	0.5	1.0	1.5	1.5	1.5	1.5	2.0	

Future contingent liability for old stock equals £9 – cost to liquidate:　　£4.5
Old stock improved during season

Trading Margin	43.30%
Future Liability	-3.00%
Resulting Margin:	40.30%

BOW = Beginning of week

Analysis of why running with too much stock causes higher markdowns and lost sales

14 Weeks' Cover Profile Week:	1	2	3	4	5	6	7	8	9	10	11	12	13	14	15	Season total:
BOW Total Stock	140	140	140	140	140	140	140	140	140	140	140	140	140	140	140	
Previous Season Stock	60	56	52	50	48	47	47	47	47	47	47	47	47	45	41	
This Season Stock	80	84	88	90	92	93	93	87	77	67	59	51	44	39	35	
Next Season Stock	0	0	0	0	0	0	0	6	16	26	34	42	49	56	64	
check	140	140	140	140	140	140	140	140	140	140	140	140	140	140	140	
Week Total Intake	10	10	10	10	10	10	10	10	10	10	10	10	10	10	10	
Previous Season Intake	0	0	0	0	0	0	0	0	0	0	0	0	0	0	0	
This Season Intake	10	10	10	10	10	10	4	0	0	0	0	0	0	0	0	
Next Season Intake	0	0	0	0	0	0	6	10	10	10	10	10	10	10	10	
check	10	10	10	10	10	10	10	10	10	10	10	10	10	10	10	
Week Total Sales	10	10	10	10	10	10	10	10	10	10	10	10	10	10	10	150.00
Previous Season Sales	4	4	2	2	1	0	0	0	0	0	0	0	2	4	3	
This Season Sales	6	6	8	8	9	10	10	10	10	8	8	7	5	4	4	
Next Season Sales	0	0	0	0	0	0	0	0	0	2	2	3	3	2	3	
check	10	10	10	10	10	10	10	10	10	10	10	10	10	10	10	
Total Cover	14	14	14	14	14	14	14	14	14	14	14	14	14	14	14	
Previous Season Cover	15.0	14.0	26.0	25.0	48.0								23.5	11.3	13.7	
This Season Cover	13.3	14.0	11.0	11.3	10.2	9.3	9.3	8.7	7.7	8.4	7.4	7.3	8.8	9.8	8.8	
Next Season Cover									13.0	17.0	14.0	16.3	28.0	21.3		
Margin Percent	30.00%	30.00%	38.00%	36.00%	42.50%	50.00%	50.00%	50.00%	45.00%	46.00%	42.00%	43.00%	30.50%	14.00%	19.00%	37.73%
Previous Season Stock	0.00%	0.00%	-10.00%	-20.00%	-25.00%								-10.00%	-20.00%	-20.00%	
This Season Stock	50.00%	50.00%	50.00%	50.00%	50.00%	50.00%	50.00%	50.00%	45.00%	45.00%	40.00%	40.00%	35.00%	30.00%	25.00%	
Next Season Stock										50.00%	50.00%	50.00%	50.00%	50.00%	50.00%	
Margin Quantum	3.0	3.0	3.8	3.6	4.3	5.0	5.0	5.0	4.5	4.6	4.2	4.3	3.1	1.4	1.9	56.60
Previous Season Stock	0.0	0.0	-0.2	-0.4	-0.3	0.0	0.0	0.0	0.0	0.0	0.0	0.0	-0.2	-0.8	-0.6	
This Season Stock	3.0	3.0	4.0	4.0	4.5	5.0	5.0	5.0	4.5	3.6	3.2	2.8	1.8	1.2	1.0	
Next Season Stock										1.0	1.0	1.5	1.5	1.0	1.5	

Total Sales 150 Ave stock 140

Opening Stock for Next Season:

76k of old stock vs 60k of old at beginning of period
Next season (new) stock at 64k vs beginning of period of 80k
Higher % of sales generated on old stock – 15.3% of sales vs 5.3% in 7 wks profile
Lower % of sales generated on new season – 10% vs 12.6% of sales in 7 wks profile
75.3% of sales on current season goods compared to 83.3% of sales in 7 wk scenario
Future contingent liability to liquidate old stock of £76k is £38k – deteriorated from liability of £30k at start of season

Trading Margin	37.73%
Future Liability	-25.33%
Resulting Margin:	12.40%

£38

Analysis of why running with too much stock causes higher markdowns and lost sales

																Season total:
21 Weeks' Cover Profile Week:	1	2	3	4	5	6	7	8	9	10	11	12	13	14	15	
BOW Total Stock	210	210	210	210	210	210	210	210	210	210	210	210	210	210	210	
Previous Season Stock	60	55	51	48	46	45	44	44	44	44	44	44	42	39	35	
This Season Stock	80	85	89	92	94	95	96	93	90	80	71	63	57	52	48	
Next Season Stock	0	0	0	0	0	0	0	3	6	16	25	33	41	49	57	
check	140	140	140	140	140	140	140	140	140	140	140	140	140	140	140	
Week Total Intake	10	10	10	10	10	10	10	10	10	10	10	10	10	10	10	
Previous Season Intake	0	0	0	0	0	0	0	0	0	0	0	0	0	0	0	
This Season Intake	10	10	10	10	10	10	10	7	7	0	0	0	0	0	0	
Next Season Intake	0	0	0	0	0	0	0	3	3	10	10	10	10	10	10	
check	10	10	10	10	10	10	10	10	10	10	10	10	10	10	10	
Week Total Sales	10	10	10	10	10	10	10	10	10	10	10	10	10	10	10	150.00
Previous Season Sales	5	4	3	2	1	1	0	0	0	0	0	2	3	4	4	
This Season Sales	5	6	7	8	9	9	10	10	10	9	8	6	5	4	3	
Next Season Sales	0	0	0	0	0	0	0	0	0	1	2	2	2	2	3	
check	10	10	10	10	10	10	10	10	10	10	10	10	10	10	10	
Total Cover	21	21	21	21	21	21	21	21	21	21	21	21	21	21	21	
Previous Season Cover	12.0	13.8	17.0	24.0	46.0	45.0					8.9	22.0	14.0	9.8	8.8	
This Season Cover	16.0	14.2	12.7	11.5	10.4	10.6	9.6	9.3	9.0	8.9	8.9	10.5	11.4	13.0	16.0	
Next Season Cover										16.0	12.5	16.5	20.5	24.5	19.0	
Margin Percent	20.00%	22.00%	27.50%	34.00%	42.00%	42.00%	50.00%	50.00%	45.00%	45.50%	42.00%	32.00%	21.50%	12.00%	10.50%	33.07%
Previous Season Stock	-10.00%	-20.00%	-25.00%	-30.00%	-30.00%	-30.00%						-10.00%	-20.00%	-25.00%	-30.00%	
This Season Stock	50.00%	50.00%	50.00%	50.00%	50.00%	50.00%	50.00%	50.00%	45.00%	45.00%	40.00%	40.00%	35.00%	30.00%	25.00%	
Next Season Stock	50.00%	50.00%	50.00%	50.00%	50.00%	50.00%	50.00%	50.00%	50.00%	50.00%	50.00%	50.00%	50.00%	50.00%	50.00%	
Margin Quantum	2.0	2.2	2.8	3.4	4.2	4.2	5.0	5.0	4.5	4.6	4.2	3.2	2.2	1.2	1.1	49.60
Previous Season Stock	-0.5	-0.8	-0.8	-0.6	-0.3	-0.3	0.0	0.0	0.0	0.0	0.0	-0.2	-0.6	-1.0	-1.2	
This Season Stock	2.5	3.0	3.5	4.0	4.5	4.5	5.0	5.0	4.5	4.1	3.2	2.4	1.8	1.2	0.8	
Next Season Stock	0.0	0.0	0.0	0.0	0.0	0.0	0.0	0.0	0.0	0.5	1.0	1.0	1.0	1.0	1.5	

Opening Stock for Next Season:

Total Sales 150   Ave stock 140

Trading Margin	33.07%
Future Liability	-27.67%
Resulting Margin:	5.40%

41.5

83k of old stock vs 60k at beginning of period – old stock up by 38%

Next season (new) stock at 57k vs beginning of period of 80k – new stock down 16.2%

Higher % of sales generated on old stock – 19.3% vs 15.3% of sales in 14 wks & 5.3% in 7 wks profile

Lower % of sales generated on new season – 8% vs 10% in 14 wks and 12.6% of sales in 7 wks profile

72.6% of sales on current season goods compared to 75.3% in 14 wks and 83.3% in 7 wks profile

Future contingent liability to liquidate old stock of 83k is 41.5k – deteriorated from liability of 38k at start of season

Future Liability of Stock:

If season above generates scanned margin of e.g. 40%, that appears to be a profit of 40 x 150 or 60 assuming all figures above at retail.

However, against this there is a contingent liability of £41.5 at retail or £21.0 at cost. If you take this off the £60 that it appears you have earned, the real profit of the season is not £60 on £150 of sales but £39 on £150 of sales, which is a margin of 26% not 40%.

My experience is that the situation of having too much stock and too old stock just gets worse and worse and worse.

A question for you:

Did you just skim over the previous three pages because they looked too complex???

If you have nothing to do at all with the amount of stock carried in your store, then, by all means, carry on reading.

If, on the other hand, you do have some control or influence on the amount of stock carried in your store, then go back and study the three tables carefully.

Although they are complex, they are not beyond the understanding of anyone who takes the time to study them and, together, they contain one of the absolute fundamentals to profitability in retailing.

Carrying more stock than you really need to support sales is one of the biggest reasons for lost profit in the retail business!

The best way to get out of trouble in the clothing business is to not get into trouble in the first place!

Clothing is a high-risk/high-reward business. You can get better and better but you can never get everything 100 per cent right.

Each season you have to take your best shot at forecasting how much you can sell and then, using that figure, work out how much you can afford to buy to support the sales and any promotion activity.

If you end up buying too much, whatever the cause, the only remedy is markdowns.

Sometimes you can get a supplier to take bad things back, especially if they are at fault. Sometimes you can get a supplier to fund markdowns, especially if you are a good customer and things don't go wrong too often.

However, 90 per cent of the time when you are in trouble with a style or a category the solution is going to be markdowns, and 90 per cent of the time you are going to have to pay for that yourself.

Hence the opening statement: careful planning to make sure you don't get into trouble in the first place is the only real cost-effective solution!

There are hundreds of ways to sell more of a good product. The only way to sell a bad product is markdowns!

Order lead times* affect order accuracy, which affects sell-through, which affects profit.

Days Lead	Order Accuracy		Assume Sell Reg Pr	Stock to Clear	50.00% Mkd to Clear	intake margin: Cost to Clear	Realised Margin	
30	90%		90%	10%	4.50%	2.25%	47.75%	
60	80%		80%	20%	9.00%	4.50%	45.50%	
70	75%		75%	25%	11.25%	5.63%	44.38%	
80	70%		70%	30%	15.00%	7.50%	42.50%	
90	65%		65%	35%	17.50%	8.75%	41.25%	
100	60%		60%	40%	20.00%	10.00%	40.00%	
110	55%		55%	45%	24.75%	12.38%	37.63%	
120	50%		50%	50%	27.50%	13.75%	36.25%	
130	45%		45%	55%	33.00%	16.50%	33.50%	
140	40%		40%	60%	36.00%	18.00%	32.00%	

*LEAD TIME IS THE NUMBER OF DAYS BETWEEN PLACING THE ORDER AND THE PRODUCT BEING DELIVERED

If you are able to shorten your order lead times and improve your accuracy, you might be able to take a lower intake margin.

Days Lead	Order Accuracy		Assume Sell Reg Pr	Stock to Clear	40.00% Mkd to Clear	intake margin: Cost to Clear	Realised Margin	
30	90%		90%	10%	4.50%	2.70%	37.30%	
60	80%		80%	20%	9.00%	5.40%	34.60%	
70	75%		75%	25%	11.25%	6.75%	33.25%	
80	70%		70%	30%	15.00%	9.00%	31.00%	
90	65%		65%	35%	17.50%	10.50%	29.50%	
100	60%		60%	40%	20.00%	12.00%	28.00%	
110	55%		55%	45%	24.75%	14.85%	25.15%	
120	50%		50%	50%	27.50%	16.50%	23.50%	
130	45%		45%	55%	33.00%	19.80%	20.20%	
140	40%		40%	60%	36.00%	21.60%	18.40%	

If you are able to do this, you might be able to give the customer a better price, higher quality or both – see the comparison below:

Days Lead	Order Accuracy		Assume Sell Reg Pr	Stock to Clear	50.00% Mkd to Clear	intake margin: Cost to Clear	Realised Margin
30	90%		90%	10%	4.50%	2.25%	47.75%
60	80%		80%	20%	9.00%	4.50%	45.50%
70	75%		75%	25%	11.25%	5.63%	44.38%
80	70%		70%	30%	15.00%	7.50%	42.50%
90	65%		65%	35%	17.50%	8.75%	41.25%
100	60%		60%	40%	20.00%	10.00%	40.00%
110	55%		55%	45%	24.75%	12.38%	37.63%
120	50%		50%	50%	27.50%	13.75%	36.25%
130	45%		45%	55%	33.00%	16.50%	33.50%
140	40%		40%	60%	36.00%	18.00%	32.00%

Cost Price:	$9.75
Retail Price:	$19.50
Sterling Price:	£13.00
(Sales 50 x 13 = 650)	

Days Lead	Order Accuracy		Assume Sell Reg Pr	Stock to Clear	40.00% Mkd to Clear	intake margin: Cost to Clear	Realised Margin
30	90%		90%	10%	4.50%	2.70%	37.30%
60	80%		80%	20%	9.00%	5.40%	34.60%
70	75%		75%	25%	11.25%	6.75%	33.25%
80	70%		70%	30%	15.00%	9.00%	31.00%
90	65%		65%	35%	17.50%	10.50%	29.50%
100	60%		60%	40%	20.00%	12.00%	28.00%
110	55%		55%	45%	24.75%	14.85%	25.15%
120	50%		50%	50%	27.50%	16.50%	23.50%
130	45%		45%	55%	33.00%	19.80%	20.20%
140	40%		40%	60%	36.00%	21.60%	18.40%

Cost Price:	$9.75
Retail Price:	$16.25
Sterling Price:	£10.83
Saving	16.67%
(Sales 80 x 10.83 - 866)	

At 120 days' lead time and 50 per cent intake margin, the price is 20 per cent higher, regular-price sales are £650 and the margin is 36.25 per cent.(£236)

At 60 days' lead time and 40 per cent intake margin, the price is 16 per cent lower, regular-price sales are £866 and the margin is 34.6 per cent. (£300)

It is well worth experimenting in your business with these dynamics.

Taking the same mark-up on everything is missing a huge profit opportunity.

You can be assured that your suppliers do not make the same margin on everything they sell to you. Also, there are lots of other factors that can affect margins, like what the situation is in your particular marketplace.

Customers have no idea what you PAID for the product and they don't care. All they care about is what THEY have to pay and what they are getting for it.

Therefore, when the market allows you a greater spread between your cost and the retail price, take it or use it as a chance to give better value for customers.

When you have to take less in order to be competitive, always choose to be competitive.

One of the signs of a rank-amateur buyer is to look at the detail of their purchase register and see the same or almost the same mark-up on everything.

Smart retailers know better than this!

Planning too aggressively can have a disastrous effect on profits . . . on the other hand planning conservatively and *beating* the plan generates more profit!

I have included previously in this book calculations that show how the percentage of stock sold at regular price affects margin dramatically.

It stands to reason therefore that if you OVER FORECAST sales on stock purchases for which you are responsible, you then increase the risk of loss to the business – trying for more ends up with less!

One of the key elements of any plan, and particularly any aggressive plan, is working out who takes the risk.

If you can get a supplier to take the risk, then an aggressive plan is not so bad. If you are dealing with short-time stock on hand (like produce), then the risk is not so bad because if it does not work you only lose a week.

However, if you are direct-sourcing things for which you are responsible, i.e. you buy them and you have to sell them with no help, then it does not pay to OVER FORECAST what you can achieve or else the risk goes up accordingly.

So the bottom line is that an ESSENTIAL element of any plan is 'WHO IS TAKING THE RISK?' Once you answer this question, you can complete the rest of the plan.

Another element of having too aggressive a plan in a direct-sourced department is the effect on open-to-buy. If you have an aggressive plan and it does not work, your future open-to-buy is shut down: this means you are STUCK with stock that did not sell (and nobody wants) and you CANNOT BUY new good stock that customers do want. This COMPOUNDS the effect of planning too aggressively.

On the next page I have provided two scenarios to compare.

	Scenario 1	Scenario 2	Variance
Last year's Sales:	500,000,000	500,000,000	0
This year's Sales Plan:	525,000,000	575,000,000	50,000,000
%:	5.0%	15.0%	
This year's Markdown Plan:	105,000,000	115,000,000	10,000,000
%:	20.0%	20.0%	0.0%
Up-front Buying Policy:	90% of sales + markdowns	90% of sales + markdowns	0
Up-front Buy Amount:	619,500,000	678,500,000	59,000,000
In-season Open-to-buy Plan:	10,500,000	11,500,000	1,000,000
Actual Sales Achieved:	550,000,000	550,000,000	0
%:	10.0%	10.0%	0
Sales Increase vs Plan:	25,000,000	−25,000,000	−50,000,000
%:	4.8%	−4.3%	−9.1%
In-season Open-to-buy revised to:	35,500,000	−13,500,000	−49,000,000
Change %:	238.1%	−217.4%	
Minimum In-season orders required:	8,000,000	8,000,000	0
Open-to-buy left for Repeats, etc:	27,500,000	−21,500,000	0
Cancellations Required:	0	21,500,000	21,500,000
Cancellations Achieved:	0	9,000,000	9,000,000
Extra Terminal Stock at season end:	0	12,500,000	12,500,000
Cost to Liquidate Extra Stock:	0	4,000,000	4,000,000

HOW PLANNING CAN AFFECT PROFIT IN CLOTHING:

Basic Assumptions:
- Actual Sales Achieved are the same in both cases.
- Open-to-buy and order-placing policies are the same in both cases.
- Stock that does not sell at regular price at the beginning sells on sale at the end – all sales in between are the same in both cases.

In Scenario 1 where the department over achieves its plan, no cancellations are required and there is open-to-buy left for opportunities in season. In Scenario 2 buyers are cancelling rather than buying.

In real life, under both these scenarios the sales would not be the same, as the department with open-to-buy would be in a position to have more wanted goods rather than digging its way out from under unsold goods. Markdowns would go down; sales and margins would go up.

In Scenario 2 there is £12.5m of extra terminal stock to deal with, which costs £4m. On this size operation this represents a margin reduction of almost one point.

The biggest difference between the two scenarios is the mode of operation and the attitude of the commercial teams. In Scenario 2 they are failing against the plan and cancelling orders – in a defensive mood. On the other hand, in Scenario 1 the buyers are optimistic, they are beating the plan, and they are looking to buy in goods rather than cancel.

With over 50 years' experience in clothing, I have learned the value of making a conservative plan and beating it. It always does better than the other way round.

This same technique will apply to other types of business as well in cases where long-range forward commitments are required.

There is a lot of retail chat about 'benchmarks' – the only benchmark that really matters is against the market leader in that particular category!

When you set your benchmarks – and this must be done
BY CATEGORY – the only worthwhile benchmark is against
the VERY BEST performer in your marketplace. Any other
benchmark is meaningless.

If you can match or beat the best performer you have a good
chance of winning.

If you cop out by rating yourself against some other arbitrarily
selected benchmark, it is not a true benchmark at all. You can
probably prove that what you are doing already is just fine, but
you are just kidding yourself.

The people to whom you are saying this rubbish might
not catch on to your comparison error but your customers
certainly will!

The idea that suppliers pay for anything is a complete myth.

It has been said that 'All the laws of economics boil down to the fact that there is no such thing as a free lunch.'

Nowhere is this better demonstrated than in the concept that a supplier is 'paying' for something – advertising, travel, markdowns or anything whatsoever.

Suppliers are in business to make money – if they don't they don't last very long. Therefore, any money they 'give' to a buyer has to be factored in to the price charged for the product. If you assume that the need of the retailer to make a profit is a **constant**, you then get to the situation that who pays for the 'free' money from the supplier is your **customers**.

I don't mean to imply that there is no such thing as good negotiation or that one buyer might not occasionally get a better deal than another buyer, but day in and day out, year in and year out, the supplier who survives gets their money from their customers and their customers (the retailers) get their money from *their* customers.

Personally what I would want from a supplier is the best possible product on time at the lowest possible cost. I would prefer not to have the cost 'loaded up' with all the extras for which they thought I might ask.

Nowhere is the fact that nothing is really free more dramatically demonstrated than in buying so-called 'consignment' or 'sale or return' product.

Many retailers fall into the trap of thinking that having product on consignment or sale or return is a great way to make money.

My own view is that this is a great way to make money for your suppliers and a great way to overcharge your customers, which in turn limits your business.

If you accept the fact that the supplier is not a charitable institution in business to support the retailer whatever the cost, you then must accept the fact that what they do has to be economic for their own business.

If they are going to be responsible for 'taking back' what does not sell at the end of your season in order to get it out of your inventory, what do you imagine they will do with the product? If they sell it at a loss, this has to be factored into the cost. If they sell it to someone else next year for less, both the storage and the loss on sale have to be factored in.

You must also realise that you have incurred the cost of packing it up and shipping it back to the supplier.

If you add up the costs of the supplier to factor in taking it back, your costs in sending it back and the supplier loss on disposal, you could easily cover the cost of marking it down and selling it to your own customers.

This also results in more sales for you and more happy customers who got a bargain.

I am always amazed at how retailers get sucked into thinking they have done a 'clever deal' by working with a supplier who takes back the leftover things that did not sell at the end of the season.

There are some fundamental differences between commercial or product-sourcing jobs and other jobs in a retail company. It is important for everyone, especially management, to recognise this.

If you look across all the various areas of the business there are always similarities and there are always differences. However, the differences between product sourcing or commercial departments and the others stand out because of the lack of control or risk involved.

All jobs involve risk, but some involve more risk than others.

For example, if you are a warehouse manager or a store manager you have risks involving your workforce, safety in the workplace, adequate service levels to your customers, control of costs, compliance with laws, standards, and even local customs and practices.

But you also have a lot of control in that most of the people who are involved work for you and need to follow your directives.

One of the reasons I speak elsewhere in the book about having confident teams in product sourcing is that they face all these risks plus others.

First of all, suppliers do not have to sell to any one retailer. Usually they have the option of deciding which retailers they want to do business with and this then becomes a competition to see who can be the best customers to the best suppliers. No matter how big or how important you think you might be, suppliers always have a choice, and especially a choice as to who will get their best service!

The next big risk faced by commercial or product-sourcing teams is the customer. Customers change their ideas fast and in the world of television, jet travel, internet, Instagram, Facebook, Twitter and WeChat, information travels around the world almost at the speed of light. This means there is always a risk that by the time your purchase reaches the stores, it may already be going out of demand.

Another risk area in today's world is the press. The press occasionally like to write good stories but dramas about food scares, health scares or an inappropriate product for children always make headlines. This is a factor that always has to be considered.

Right now, you may be asking yourself: 'Why is Hoerner including this? It is all blindingly obvious!' However, it might not be as obvious as you think. My experience is that in most retail organisations a real understanding of how it is not that easy for commercial people (buyers) to 'control' an outcome is sometimes rarer than it should be.

As discussed elsewhere, when something goes wrong fix it right away – this does not necessarily include blaming the buyer in all cases.

Chapter 4

MARKETING, PR & COMMUNICATIONS

Your restaurant will not be a very big success if no one knows about it. You have spent so much time and effort creating the perfect dish – how will anyone know?

'Your PR is not what you say you are; it is what you really are.'

To run one ad and assume that even 20 per cent of your customers see it or read it – let alone react to it – is incredibly naive.

Multimedia exposure (including digital), repetition and strong visual impact in every store are essential if you have a story to tell.

But, in the final analysis, there is no substitute

for personal contact with the customer by a well-informed sales associate.

If I had a limited budget, I would always do the job properly in-store first before purchasing media advertising.

However, digital media is now changing all the rules – your online presence is part of your store!

Digital media – Facebook, Twitter, and all the rest, combined with smartphones – are changing all the rules. By the time you read this, it will already be out of date!

E-COMMERCE SPEED OF CHANGE IS SCARY

- There are 6.8 billion people on the planet: 4 billion use mobile phones but only 3.5 billion have a toothbrush.

- Ninety-one per cent of adults keep their mobile phone within arm's reach 24/7.

- Twenty-five per cent of Americans use only mobile devices to access the internet.

- There are five times as many mobiles as PCs.

- Mobile phones have overtaken PCs as the most common internet-access device. Half the mobile phones in the USA and UK are smartphones.

- Sixty per cent of internet users say they expect a site to load on their phone in three seconds; 74 per cent wait only five seconds or they leave.

- Ninety-five per cent of smartphone users look up local information, 61 per cent ring as a result and 59 per cent visit as a result. This activity is expected to grow by 70 per cent in the UK in five years – the total market won't grow that much so consider impact on stores.

- Forty-five per cent of people in the UK buy something online at least once a week.

- Smartphone ownership amongst 16–30-year-olds in China is 85 per cent.

- Based on the one billion users recently announced, if Facebook were a country it would now be the third largest in the world, behind China (1.34 billion) and India (1.2 billion).

- Some observers think Twitter will overtake Facebook!

If you want to test a written communication that goes to a large number of stores, show it to a 12-year-old and ask them to explain what it means.

This is not because they are 12 – 12-year-olds are just as intelligent as adults – it is because they will be honest with you if they don't understand it!

Adults will try to bluff their way through, thinking there is something wrong with them if they don't understand it when really the problem is that **your** communication is not clear.

The more people you are writing to and the more chance for misinterpretation in either content or tone, the more time you should spend getting it exactly right.

Writing for popular consumption is an art form that too few bosses ever take the trouble to learn.

There is a good reason why the *Daily Mail* or *Sun* newspapers sells many times the number of copies of *The Times* or the *Daily Telegraph* and it is not just the gossip columns or the Page Three girls.

I have been interested to note over recent years that *The Times* and the *Telegraph* have made a huge transformation in becoming more 'reader-friendly'.

'Be the first, be the best or be the cheapest' is an old retailing adage.

I say: 'Be second, be really good and be the best value.'

The old adage 'Be the first, be the best or be the cheapest' identifies some very good points but is an over simplification and probably misleading if you are running a business of any size.

Being 'first' is exciting but probably not a good idea unless you are a very small, specialist business. It is much better to sense all the trends and get in quickly on the ones that are catching on.

Having the 'best' in your stock is very prestigious and personally satisfying but, again, unless you are running a very small business you probably cannot achieve it and even if you could most customers probably could not afford it. However, you can be 'really good' and this will set you above most of your competitors.

Lastly, the 'cheapest' is almost never the best value. Just because customers have little money does not mean they have little intelligence. They do recognise value – however, they also have to be able to afford it.

So, give the best quality you can at the price your customer can afford to pay: that is true value for money.

The best benchmark is the market leader in that particular category. They must be doing something right in order to gain that much customer support. (see page 94.)

Chapter 5

STRATEGY

Good 'scratch' cooks can whip up a delicious meal from whatever they find in the refrigerator but a really great chef plans ahead for the menu, the ingredients, how and when it will be prepared, and how and when it will be served.

To develop a good retail strategy requires hard work, brilliant thinking, careful timing and extensive research. To execute it requires making it so simple that a child could do it.

A good plan is the same set of rules, plans, budgets, people, actions and principles by which you would describe a successful operation if it had already been completed. Nothing less can be called a real plan.

Any management team is a lot more enthusiastic and effective in implementing a strategy that they helped to develop themselves . . . and, it is also very likely to be a better strategy!

If you can engineer it so that the team you expect to deliver a strategy can participate in developing it, you not only get a better strategy and a more willing group of champions for it but you are very likely to have a strategy that is less prone to disappointments.

Almost everyone gives lip service to the concept of participation but very few people really do it. There is a great tendency for bosses to decide what to do, and then try to figure out effective ways of getting people to do it.

My experience is that what you as the boss should decide is what you want to get DONE, which is something quite different from what to DO.

Once you know what you want to get DONE, you can then freely involve your senior team to help you decide what to DO in order to get it done.

You are the boss – you are in charge of the questions. If you determine the right questions, your team should be able to come up with the right answers.

At first, this process may seem like it will take a lot longer and be cumbersome. However, my experience is that it saves loads of time and is considerably more effective.

On the following page I will give a sample outline of how such a process might be structured.

Step 1 – Decide what you want to get done.

Step 2 – Six or more weeks ahead, set the planning day aside in a quiet setting – a day when everyone can and will be there.

Step 3 – Break the aspects down into three or four questions to be answered. For example, how big a factor is Facebook or Twitter in communication with customers now? What is it likely to be in five years? What examples are there of others who are already using it? What can we learn from this and what should we do about it?

Step 4 – Break your team down into three or four groups (with a minimum of two and maximum of five people per group) to answer the questions.

Step 5 – Announce the agenda once groups are assigned.

Agenda:

- Opening 30 minutes

- Four sessions – 1 hour each (30 minutes' presentation; 30 minutes' discussion)

- Break for lunch

- Revisit each topic for 30–45 minutes to come to conclusions about actions, ways forward, next steps, who will do what.

- Closing and summary

- End of day or dinner with the team

There are lots of variations on the above but the important aspect is that the team will develop what to DO about what you have decided needs to be DONE.

Everyone knows you cannot manage 'outputs' – you have to manage 'inputs'. But … you have to understand what the outputs really are before you can adjust the inputs successfully.

'We must form perfect models in thought and look at them continually or we will never carve them out into grand and noble lives.'

Mary Baker Eddy, Founder of Christian Science, 1866

'If you don't know where you are going, any road will get you there!'

Redmond J. Largay, President and CEO of Associated Dry Goods, 1982

'The only way to hit an invisible target is by accident!'

Julia Cook, CEO Change Management Group, 2011

One of the absolute fundamentals of having a good strategy and leading the organisation to achieve that strategy is for everyone to know exactly where you are going.

This does NOT mean you have to always know exactly **how** you will get there . . . that is a great help, of course, but it is not required.

What **is required** is a clear picture of where you are going, and by picture I mean in relation to all aspects of the business – customers, suppliers, retail environment, merchandise presentation techniques, customer policies, product strategy, finance, necessary approvals and, above all, the people who will be required to carry all this out.

Strategies fail time after time because they are not thought through well enough.

When I became head of the Burton Group in 1992 we gathered all the senior people in a room for two days and talked through where we were and where we were going. We created the road map for the recovery of the company.

By the time I joined Tesco Clothing in 2000 I had learned a lot more about how this works. This time we brought the senior team together for as long as it took to map out exactly the vision of what we wanted to offer customers in three years' time. This took a lot of time but it was worth it.

Our vision covered every aspect of the business, including: merchandise fashionability, quality, return policies, fixtures, advertising, fitting rooms, supplier policies, pricing policies, how the department in the store would look, and how customers would feel when they shopped there. Of course, we worked within financial parameters but the key to developing our successful business was developing a vision – which everyone could imagine, just like watching a movie – of what it would be like to be a customer shopping in the department. We could see what would be for sale, and how it would be serviced and presented, and therefore we could figure out what it would take to accomplish the vision.

It worked. Within a year we had rebuilt the clothing department. We had introduced new suppliers who had the right equipment and standards to produce the garments we needed; we had trained staff who could merchandise clothing rails as competently as they could fill shelves and fresh-fruit fixtures; we had new fitting rooms; we had launched a new brand called Cherokee. This was the underpinning for doubling sales, which we achieved in the anticipated time frame.

The ability to have a clear vision of where you are going and to share this with your team in a way that they can all understand is an absolute essential of leadership.

Most people come to work wanting to do a good job. If they are not being effective, there is a very good chance that one reason for this is that they don't understand completely what they are supposed to be doing.

Change management *is* management.

It does not take much effort to just keep doing the same thing on and on and over and over. Any business has to grow and change with the times. If you do not, you wake up to find that the world has passed you by.

Therefore, the ability to lead change is an essential part of leadership.

In order to lead change, you have to have the following in place:

1. You have to have a clear vision of where you are now and where you want to go.
2. The team has to understand this fully and buy into it, hopefully, as discussed earlier, because they helped to develop the plan themselves.
3. Each key person has to understand fully what their part is: scope, timing, interaction.
4. You have to engage with all the others that are affected by the change you want to make – other departments, divisions, companies, customers, shareholders, bankers, and so on.
5. You have to have the resources to do the job. You cannot expect people to have unlimited additional capacity without it affecting their main job.
6. You have to have the budget.
7. You have to have a clear plan with milestones that measure progress – milestones that everyone understands and to which they agree.
8. You have to be willing to change the plan when parts of it are not working.
9. You have to celebrate success when things are working.

The above words are so simple but simple and easy are not the same thing. In fact, leading change is one of the hardest things to do because people are creatures of habit.

People are often comfortable with their current activities, jobs, relationships, etc. Change is hard, scary and can sometimes be threatening as well. Never underestimate the fact that people will always behave in what they PERCEIVE to be their own best interest. This does not mean their perception is correct but it does govern behaviour.

Of all the tests of leadership of which I can think, leading a big change programme is about the toughest. It is easier when people or the company are under threat. It is much harder when people perceive that what is going on now is just fine and see no real reason to change. That is where the shared vision comes in – go back to points 1 and 2 – a clear shared vision of where you are going and why it is essential to make all the rest of the plan work.

However good you think your plan is, and however good you think you are at it, you should realise that it will probably take a little longer and cost a little more than you imagined at the outset. Don't let this come as a shock. Direction is always more important than speed!

Plan for success . . .

But be ready to change the plan when required.

Some people say plan for the worst and hope for the best but this does not work. You have to plan for success.

Elsewhere in this book we have discussed change and planning, and what that takes. The point here is that retailing is a business that has to be positive.

Because it is a risk business and the teams are constantly making bets on what will sell and when and at what price, an attitude of optimism is required to approach the business from the right perspective.

Therefore any planning you do **has to be a plan for success**!

If for some reason the plan is not working, then change it – but make sure it is always a move in a positive direction.

HEALTH WARNING ON BUDGETS AND FINANCE:

Every business has elaborate accounting systems and staff to track and control every one of their expenses down to the last penny

except there is
no expense line
for the biggest
expense of all –
lost opportunity.
It is the job of
management to be
able to calculate the
cost of *not* doing
things along with the
cost of doing them!

A good example of this is the cost of store staffing. The finance department always knows exactly how much it costs. They have no way of knowing how much business you lose if you don't spend the money.

Another example is communication with stores. In one company for which I worked the programme of two way stores communication and contact was eliminated to 'save money'. The amount of money saved was in the hundreds of thousands. The cost of saving this money was in the millions.

Another example is buyer travel. People in finance departments who never go anywhere are keen to point out how much it costs to send a buyer to buy or to go on a fashion-sample shopping trip. What they have no way of calculating or factoring in is the value to the business of the buyer having the knowledge and the information to make a better buy, which results in more sales and a greater margin.

It is a management job – one of the most important – to make sure that we don't save pennies and lose pounds.

Chapter 6

INVESTMENT VS EXPENSE

Are you 'spending money' or 'investing money'? There is a huge difference!

WHEN IT COMES TO
INVESTING MONEY IN A
RETAIL BUSINESS, THE
DECK IS STACKED
AGAINST SOME
IMPORTANT THINGS
THAT REALLY MATTER.
YOU SHOULD WATCH
OUT FOR THIS IF YOU
ARE THE BOSS (OR IF
YOU ARE NOT THE BOSS
AND ARE SUFFERING
THE CONSEQUENCES!).

There are two big factors that stack the deck. The first is
generally accepted accounting practices. The second is
substantial resources in companies outside the business
that gain big revenue from selling things to retailers. There
is a third factor that sometimes comes into play and that is
the desire in all businesses for 'instant gratification'. All three
factors play a role in disturbing the balance of investment
away from things that really matter.

'GENERALLY ACCEPTED ACCOUNTING PRACTICES'

According to accounting rules, there are certain things that qualify for 'capital investment' – things like new computer systems or building stores or warehouses. These can then be 'written off' over time – maybe five, ten or even twenty years.

The effect of this means that if you spend £1,000,000 on building a store and write this off over 20 years, the charge to profit is only £50,000 per year.

If you spend £500,000 on fixtures and fittings and write this off over seven years, the charge to profit is only £71,500 per year.

On the other hand, if you invest in a buying team to upgrade a product range and this costs £200,000, the entire £200,000 is a charge to profit in that year.

This distortion in accounting rules between so-called 'revenue charges' (things you have to pay for right away) and capital investment tends to make it easier for management to spend large sums of money on systems, real estate, stores, fixtures, etc., and make it harder for them to invest in people and talent within their own organisation.

In my view this always puts 'people investment' at a disadvantage against investment in systems and stores. And, it gets worse – see the next page.

IN ADDITION TO THE ACCOUNTING FACTOR, THERE ARE VAST RESOURCES WORKING TO CHANNEL INVESTMENT INTO SYSTEMS AND STORES.

Companies who sell systems or construction to retailers make a lot of money. Their entire income stream depends on selling big projects to retailers and they invest in this heavily, both in people and money, to get their point across.

This force, when combined with the capital expenditure accounting rules discussed above, adds another heavy weighting in favour of retailers investing in systems and construction rather than people.

There is no organisation or budget devoted to putting forward the advantages of investing in people.

There is no way to write off the investment in people over time, even though this investment might not pay off for a year or two.

People investment has to be managed from within the company by those who are smart enough to realise the value of investing in talent as well as systems and construction.

THE NATURAL HUMAN DESIRE FOR INSTANT GRATIFICATION ALSO PLAYS A ROLE.

If you build a beautiful store, you can see it right away as soon as it is finished. If you re-fit an old store with new furniture, fixtures and fittings, you can see it right away when it opens.

If you install a new system (which does take time) you tend to think it is done when it goes live. (Even though real benefits may come through over time – or never.)

On the other hand investment in people, especially commercial talent, sometimes takes quite a while to mature. In my experience it usually provides almost no benefit the first year, a little in the second year and really starts to pay off in the third year.

Investment in store staffing pays off almost instantly once the people are trained and operating.

Investment in promotional advertising usually pays off right away – or it should. However, investment in 'brand building' can be very long-range: it can take up to five years before the results really start to come through.

Experienced retail bosses are always conscious of the fact that some forms of what are called 'revenue expenses' in accounting are really 'investments' that take time to pay off.

Chapter 7

PEOPLE

Who is in the kitchen and how good are they? Who is serving and how good are they? Can you ever imagine a really great restaurant being run without the people who make it what it is?

How to interview a prospective employee:

It is quite arrogant to imagine that in 30 or 45 minutes you can assess whether or not someone is qualified to do a job. Many times people – both the prospective employee and the interviewer – are not 100 per cent candid in interviews. So how do you get the right information exchange in an interview?

1. Be open and frank. What you *can* do is be 100 per cent frank about the job itself, including all the pitfalls and problems. The person may not choose to reveal their true self to you but they know themselves and the more you tell them about the bad side of the job, the greater the chance they will take themselves out of the running if they really aren't the right person.

2. You can tell if you like the person or not. Long ago I stopped hiring people I did not like – I learned that no one else liked them either!

3. Take references yourself. It amazes me that many people spend a long time interviewing and then leave reference checking to a headhunter or the HR department.

If the job is important, get a couple of references from the prospect and talk to the referees yourself. Referees will say 121 things to you on the phone that they wouldn't necessarily say to a third party or put in writing.

How to know if you have hired the right person after they start:

Even the best interview process is flawed and a hit rate of 70 per cent is really good. The way you find out early on if you have hired the right person is to watch what they work on.

If they get busy on the job at hand, figure out what needs to be done and either get on with it or come up with recommendations to check with you, you have a winner.

If they examine everything and pitch up with a list of what other people need to do first in order for them to be successful, the chances are you have hired a dud. Or, if they decide after a few days that they want to do something different and try to redefine their job from the one you hired them to do, watch out!

In the case of someone in a management position, also watch how they treat their own people. If they make an effort to get to know them and understand what they do, you have a winner. If they spend all their time on politics and sucking up to the boss to the exclusion of their own team time, watch out!

When you boil it all down, what you should really look for in people is integrity.

This is the ability and the courage to admit it when you are wrong.

'If you don't have that, not much else matters.'

Sir John Hoskyns, Chairman of the Burton Group

When I first worked with John Hoskyns at the Burton Group I quickly learned that he had appreciation for all types of people from all walks of life and with all types of skills. It is possible he learned this in his military career as well as in building a successful business.

In all businesses, no matter how big or how small, people make mistakes. This is not the issue. It is what they do about them that matters, and I have learned over the years that what John said about personal integrity and being able to admit when you are wrong is a key indicator of success in business.

I have seen a lot of successful people who have this quality. I have seen a lot of people fail who do not.

It is not something you can learn in a training course – people either have it or they do not and it was probably instilled at an early age.

The more organised and efficient you are during business hours, the more important it is to give your direct team some 'agenda-free' time.

If you are a relaxed type of manager with plenty of free time and an open door, this section is not for you.

If you, like most people in retailing, have more to do in a day than you can possibly get done and you are moving rapidly from one project or meeting to another, then it is important, once in a while, to give the key members of your team some 'agenda-free' time.

I usually try to have lunch out (during business hours) with people who have family obligations and plan dinners with those whose personal schedules are more flexible.

The idea is to change the environment from normal hectic office discourse (which is usually about an agenda) and give the colleague time to talk about whatever they think is important.

For this to work effectively, you have to make a special effort NOT to have an agenda of your own. Wait, listen and see what happens. Invariably, whenever I have taken the time to do this, I have learned something important.

This also builds a different type of relationship with your team. They see you as someone that gives time and listens, and you learn about their interests and concerns.

It's best to make it an early dinner – and don't go out drinking afterwards!

Good people are best motivated when they take full responsibility for their area – whatever that may be – this works at all levels of the business.

IT IS CALLED EMPOWERMENT!

The leader's secret to empowering teams while still keeping control is FREEDOM WITHIN A FRAMEWORK. I first learned about this from a management consultant, Norman Strauss, who was immensely helpful in my early days at the Burton Group.

It is the job of the leader to set out what needs to be accomplished in the context of the business. To motivate teams to achieve the goal, people in the teams (at whatever level) need to participate in figuring out how to 'get it done'.

If the teams help create the path to achievement then they will feel a sense of ownership over both the plan and the goal. They will also understand in detail what they need to get done and feel determined to meet their targets.

In order for teams to feel confident, and for their leader to feel comfortable that they can 'let go' and trust the teams to deliver responsibly, boundaries must be set. Boundaries can be specific or general or financial or subjective; in fact boundaries must be *both* specific and general, and they must be *both* financial and subjective.

Examples of boundaries:

- Operate within the budget – business-plan boundary
- Keep faith with how we treat customers – integrity and culture boundary
- Keep faith with how we treat suppliers – integrity and culture boundary
- Keep faith with how we treat our own people – integrity and culture boundary
- Obey the laws in the country in which we operate – integrity and social responsibility boundary

Once the team has come up with the plan with your agreement and support, and the boundaries are clear, let the team operate and deliver within that plan and take FULL RESPONSIBILITY for the outcomes. This not only is **motivating** but it puts you, the leader, in the strongest possible position to **monitor** performance.

If you meddle, fiddle, constantly supervise and tell people what to do, then performance becomes muddled as 'your performance' rather than theirs. Team members become passengers on a train that you are driving and you lose the motivational power of them taking responsibility.

I don't accept the view that people are lazy and don't want responsibility. It is my experience that they thrive on it. However, if the chance to feel truly responsible is taken away from them, they turn off, lose interest in their jobs and only do enough to get by and 'follow orders'.

Successful retailing requires innovation and risk taking. People are only CONFIDENT to take risks and innovate when they feel secure in their jobs and are not constantly looking over their shoulder in case they get second-guessed.

This technique of 'freedom within a framework' builds your team's confidence in you and your confidence in them. They know where the boundaries are.

By the way, this technique also works with dogs, young children and teenagers!

People who have too many things to do have a tendency to choose their own priorities within the long list. The result is that management loses control of the priorities.

DON'T GIVE YOUR TEAM TOO MANY PRIORITIES AT ONCE

The completely hypothetical grid opposite attempts to demonstrate visually what happens within a functioning team when they are given too many things to do. Even though they may be willing to work extra hours, this cannot go on forever and there is never enough time to do all that should be done. The result is that people become unhappy and begin to set their own priorities within the list of those on their inbox.

The numbers are all notional and you can substitute any numbers you like but the overall effect demonstrated is still the same.

The positive effect of the extra work put in by the team is lost due to inefficiency, confusion and frustration.

It is an important principle of good leadership to be conscious of how the workload is affecting the team and to make sure that not too many priorities are dumped on them at once.

There is always a little spare capacity within any group but, depending on by how much, when this capacity is exceeded things start to come apart.

HOW STRESSED TEAMS COPE	Normal	Stress Level 1	Stress Level 2	Stress Level 3	Percentages are notional – it is the principles and the trend that are being illustrated
Doing the day job	51%	41%	31%	25%	Half the time previously spent on the main job
Fixing things that went wrong	15%	20%	25%	30%	Twice the time fixing problems
Planning for the future	15%	12%	10%	6%	Planning time down 60% – affects future business
Positive social contact/networking	15%	12%	10%	5%	Job not as much fun – morale
Frustration time (alone or in groups)	2%	3%	8%	15%	Not positive or productive – extra time invested is wasted
Complaining	2%	3%	5%	10%	Not positive or productive – extra time invested is wasted
Looking for another job	0%	2%	5%	8%	Risk of losing good colleagues to competitors
The first additional project or situation		15%	10%	7%	Project suffers with additions
The second project or situation			12%	8%	Project never gets the effort required so suffers
The third project or situation				10%	Project never gets the effort required so suffers
Hours required to get the job done	100%	108%	116%	124%	The longer this goes on the worse the effect gets
MAIN JOB POSITIVE SUB-TOTAL	96%	85%	76%	66%	Positive work on main job now down by a third
NEGATIVE ACTIVITY SUB-TOTAL	4%	8%	18%	33%	Eight times increase in time spent on negative activity
ADDED PROJECT SUB-TOTAL	0%	15%	22%	25%	

Normal means a happy, adequately resourced functioning team

Stress Level 1: given a project or situation that requires 15% additional activity (effort or time) than normal

Most teams can handle this easily

Stress Level 2: another project or situation is added on top of the previous one, requiring another 15% effort or time

The stress starts to show!

Stress Level 3: yet another project or situation is added on top of the previous two, requiring another 15% effort or time

Things start to fall apart!

People who have too many things to do tend to set their own priorities within that list. This is a dangerous situation because the leadership then loses control of the business priorities.

The difficulty of getting busy people together in one place at one time increases in line with the square of the number of people involved.

My experience is that when you are trying to organise getting people together all in one place at one time for more than an hour or **especially when travel is involved**, the difficulty of doing this goes up in line with the square of the number of people involved.

If getting 2 people together takes 2 days, getting 3 people together takes 9 days, getting 4 people together takes 16 days, and 10 up to around 3 months' lead time. This may sound either overly dramatic or simplistic but I first had this thought about 25 years ago and it has proven to be true again and again over all that time.

If you are the boss, I don't advise it, but you can always shorten this by **bullying** people to change their schedules at the expense of your reputation, their efficiency and their relationship with you.

However, if you are trying to organise people who don't report to you or you care about your reputation, the only solution is to start way ahead of time.

If the people who work for you have schedules that are so loose that they can accommodate significant chunks of time at short notice, you might start thinking about whether or not you really need them all!

Many people go through their entire careers without ever figuring this out and the cost to them is both in the efficiency of their own staff and their own reputation.

If the boss allows poor performers to survive, it means the best people have to work harder or the team produces less – or both. What's fair about that?

There can be many reasons why a person is not performing their job. These might include:

1. They have health problems.
2. They have personal problems.
3. They are not smart enough.
4. They don't have the right experience.
5. They are lazy or don't want to work hard enough.
6. They have a problem accepting authority or direction.

The point is that while the causes or combinations of causes are many and varied **the effect on the business is the same**.

One of the big differences between American and English business culture is in dealing with poor performance. It is one of the few areas where I personally have found that the American approach is much better and more effective.

English culture does not like 'confrontation' of any kind. Therefore, talking to someone about their performance and what they might do to improve it is almost forbidden territory. The usual way is to go along for a year or two and then have a purge for 'expense reasons' during which time all the dodgy performers can be made 'redundant'. This way all confrontation is avoided, 'nothing to do with you', etc., and everyone can feel that somehow 'fate' is responsible.

The American culture, the one I believe is better, means people are entitled all the time to know how they are doing – good, bad or indifferent! (Also see the section on dogs later in the chapter.)

There is a prescribed way to have this conversation that I have found works effectively:

Conversation No. 1:

1. Review the expectations of the business – this should already have been agreed long ago. If it has not it is your fault and you have to start there first!
2. Review the performance compared to these expectations – give specific examples.
3. Get their agreement that the performance is a shortfall.
4. Get their suggestions as to what should be done about it.
5. Agree on the improvement plan, timescale and monitoring process you will both use.
6. Follow through with the monitoring process.

The above should be effective in bringing about the desired change in a short time frame. However, if it does not, you will have to move on to . . .

Conversation No. 2:

1. Review Conversation No. 1.
2. Point out that change has not taken place, despite your agreement and subsequent monitoring reviews.
3. State that the business requires change to take place and this will take the form of them changing their approach or perhaps you having to get someone else to do the job if they are unable to change.
4. Review precisely what they have to start doing.
5. Review precisely what they have to stop doing.
6. Agree on a timescale and monitoring process for 4 and 5 above.
7. At this point, I usually end with something like: 'I will support you through this process. I would *like* to tell you that I am optimistic that it will work out – but based upon the fact that we have had this conversation before and the change has not happened, I am not optimistic. You will have to try very hard to make these changes. You should also consider whether or not this is the right job for you.'

The follow-on to the first conversation can be measured and take time. The follow-on to the second has to be short and sharp. You have to be prepared to move quickly if there is not a marked change because you already have a bad apple in your barrel.

When it comes to Conversation No. 2, I always write it down carefully. When the meeting starts, I say, 'This is an important meeting. It is so important that I have written down what I want to say to you and at the end of the meeting I will give you a copy.' Sometimes seeing it in black and white does the job of getting through better than a conversation.

Please note: **Never ever** give a salary rise to someone who is underperforming. It sends entirely the wrong message. Save the money to go along with the encouraging comments when the improvement comes!

HEALTH WARNING: The above advice is derived from 56 years' practical experience in several different countries. In today's regulatory world, employment law and company policy dictate the rules and you will, of course, have to follow that law and policy in any case where it conflicts with the advice I have given above.

Don't **be** tough – but know how to **get** tough when the situation demands it.

'Speak softly and carry a big stick.'
US President Teddy Roosevelt

See the sections in this chapter on confidence and how to motivate people and you will see the wisdom of the idea that being a tough, scary boss is not a good way to get people on board with what you are trying to get done.

On the other hand, you must always be ready, when required, to 'get' tough.

The atmosphere in your business should be as follows:

When you do good things, lots of good things happen.

When you make a mistake, you learn from it and move on.

When you make the same mistake over again, something bad happens.

Another related principle is:

'Everyone has the right to **make** mistakes – they don't have the right to **procrastinate** about fixing them!'

Joseph Noble, Retail Consultant, 1961

In the right, confident atmosphere, mistakes can be admitted and fixed. What should be heavily discouraged, if not punished, is covering up or procrastinating about fixing the mistake.

I can't think of any time in my entire business experience when a mistake automatically fixed itself. I can think of plenty of times when not acting quickly enough to fix a mistake cost us a lot of money!

PEOPLE LEARN
THE FASTEST
AND REMEMBER
WHAT THEY
HAVE LEARNED
THE LONGEST
WHEN THEY ARE
HAVING FUN.

According to many studies done on how people learn (and this applies to dogs, too, by the way), learning is fastest, most effective and retained the longest when it is fun.

This is why I have a low level of interest in training courses.

They are only appropriate for basic skills like learning how to run a till.

In 99 per cent of cases, a meeting or a workshop environment where everyone participates and develops the outcome together gives the best result.

It is sometimes thought that workshops and seminars are appropriate for very 'senior' people and that junior people should just be 'trained'.

My experience has been that this view is rubbish.

Any person – whatever age – is subject to being seduced by having fun. In education studies of situations where students sit in a classroom and just listen, the retention rate of what the teacher taught (or thinks they taught) is as low as 15 per cent.

On the other hand, in an activity where there is participation and involvement and fun, the retention rate goes up substantially.

The basic makeup of all human beings is pretty much the same.

Before you plan a 'training' course, think about how you would like to spend the day yourself – sitting in a chair being 'talked at' or participating in a game or a workshop.

When two members of the same team escalate a conflict between them to 'win-lose' status, they both lose and the team loses!

'My enemy's enemy is my friend.'

There is nothing more debilitating to a smooth-running successful team than when two of the members develop a personal conflict between them.

It gets worse if this escalates to the level where it interferes with their effectiveness and is concerning and disruptive to other team members.

The solution I have found most effective is what I call the 'greater common enemy' approach.

When something like this comes up, I make it my business to become a bigger consideration/problem to **both** of them than they could ever be to each other. They must quickly learn that they will have to work together if they want to stay on the team.

If they don't learn this pretty quick, I would get rid of both of them – no matter how effective or valuable they think they are because a confident team working together toward common goals is what delivers results.

A CONFIDENT TEAM IS A REQUIREMENT FOR SUCCESSFUL RETAILING.

All retailing, from a cart vendor in Bangkok to a big international retailer like Tesco or Wal-Mart, is a risk business.

As soon as you have committed to a product, your sales and profitability depends upon your ability to sell it.

If you require everything you do to be 100 per cent guaranteed by suppliers, then they are making profit that could be yours.

The trick is to take a 'controlled' and 'calculated' risk and the job of your team is to control and calculate it!

This is where the confidence comes in. If your team lives in constant fear of making a mistake (something I have run into all too often) then their entire attitude is defensive and concentrates on avoiding any possible situation where something could go wrong or they could get the 'blame'.

This eats up a huge amount of unproductive time.

This is morale-destroying.

This means you miss out on new developments in the marketplace that could benefit or create excitement for customers.

A confident team is 99 per cent of the time a good team.

A scared team is 99 per cent of the time falling way short of what they could be doing for the customer.

If I had someone working for me that I could not fully support and help them to feel totally confident, I would make it possible for them to work elsewhere. There is absolutely no benefit to the business from any 'threatening' type of leadership.

If you have to threaten your staff to get them to perform there is something wrong with them and something very wrong with your leadership.

A person is not
ready for promotion
if they do not enjoy
the respect of their
peers.

A 'support group'
is necessary for
any executive to
function
successfully.

Promotion of a person who has the respect of the organisation enhances morale.*

(*The *contrapositive* of this is usually even truer, i.e. promoting people who do not enjoy respect is extremely demoralising to the organisation!)

Spending time developing your team is an investment that pays off in future results.

You should have unlimited time to invest but no time to waste.

The difference
between investing
and wasting is in
how many times
you have to
have the same
conversation.

It might be obvious, but one way to advance your career is to avoid aggravating your boss.

Here are some tips on how you can be guaranteed **to aggravate your boss** and then you can avoid them!

1. Keep everything to yourself. Above all, never ask their advice or they will find out how little you know.

2. Continue to work on the projects you are given right up to the last minute. Don't involve them at all along the way. Then, present the finished product for approval just before the deadline and tell them they have to approve it right away, that if they make any changes this will delay the project. This delay then will be their fault.

3. Be secretive about your whereabouts. Disappear without trace from time to time. This will keep them on their toes.

4. If you disagree with a policy, a programme or a directive, never discuss it with them. Discuss it with everyone else in your department and, if possible, a few people in other departments. That way you or your boss will not have to directly face up to any of the issues.

5. Wait until the day before they are getting ready to go on holiday and ring up with an urgent list of things to go over. That will guarantee that they won't be spending too much time on them or with you.

6. Never ask a sticky question on a Friday when they will have time to think about it over the weekend. Hit them on Monday morning along with everybody and everything else.

7. If you disagree with your boss, be sure to speak up in meetings, that way everyone will know how brave and intelligent you are and how the boss got it wrong. On the other hand, if they ever accidentally get something right, be sure to give this feedback in private.

8. Tell their secretary you need to see them but don't tell them what it is about – that way they won't be able to do something more important or urgent instead. (See my rules for organising my time later in this chapter – I never allow anyone to make an appointment for me unless I know what it is about!)

Most people have no idea of how big a factor 'luck' plays in finding a new job – they also have no idea about how hard they need to work at it.

Finding a new job is very important for lots of reasons. Yet, it always surprises me how few people really understand how the job market works or how hard they need to work to really get the best possible opportunity.

Almost everyone knows the importance of having a good CV and it is easy to get lots of advice on this. However, what is not so well-known is the significance of the 'cover letter', which must be tailored to the target organisation or company. The whole purpose of the cover letter is to get them to read the CV.

There are six hurdles that have to be overcome on the way to a successful new job. Each one depends on the step above.

1. You must have an impressive CV.
2. You must have a good cover letter tailored to the prospect.*
3. There has to be a suitable job open.
4. You have to be invited for and have a successful interview.
5. You have to be the best candidate.
6. You have to want to accept the terms and conditions offered or which can be negotiated.

Considering all the possibilities for the process to go wrong, the best recipe for success is to cast your net much wider than you think you should: 50 or 100 prospects are much more likely to gain you success than 10!

(*Addressed properly to a real person with the correct title and name spelled correctly!)

The bigger and more important your job is, the more important it is for you to organise your personal time.

(This also applies if you aspire to have a bigger and more important job!)

BACKGROUND

In your previous jobs you may have had a single-function job –
maybe it was complex but basically one function.

Now, as part of a large, complex retail organisation, you will
have multi-responsibilities.

In addition to supervising your own team, you must also
maintain good working relations and effective ways of
efficiently working with other departments.

This is a *far* different type of job and it can eat up time to the
point where you find it difficult to do the job that you were hired
to do.

Therefore, personal time management and organisation of
time, and avoiding **wasting** time, is a key factor to success or
even survival in the large-store environment.

What I have done here is try to jot down a few of the ideas
I have found to work over the years in order to make my use
of time more efficient. I hope you find at least some of them
helpful.

Even if you think some of this sounds a bit crazy, they have
worked for me for over 50 years – so you might consider trying
them for a couple of weeks to see how you get on. You could
always revert to your previous habits any time you like.

Rule 1 – TAKE CHARGE OF YOUR OWN TIME

The first step is you have to *take control* of your time. Don't let *other* people control your time – you do it.

Make a new pact with your PA – they can no longer book appointments for you; they can 'provisionally' book them but will have to 'check with you first'. Also, people cannot ask for 'time' – they have to ask for a meeting for a purpose and they have to tell the PA what it is. If they won't tell them then the PA will not make the provisional appointment (unless it is a personal matter). A couple of times a day they review the requests with you and you validate the importance and use of time based on what the subject is.

Teach your team not to waste your time – they have to come to the meeting prepared. I usually give people half or a maximum of 75 per cent of the amount of time they ask for; if they say they need an hour, tell them you only have a half-hour and they will have to be organised to get it done in that time. They spend more time getting ready and you save your time. It also helps them to think better and more clearly.

Make another pact with your secretary: they keep a reporter's notebook (spiral top) and write down everything you ask them to do permanently in this book. They cross off each thing when they get it done and give the date – you can always refer back to this record. Keep the old notebooks. That way you don't have to follow up on the PA – they follow up on themselves. Make it part of their job to follow up on themselves and on you!

Don't book yourself up too tightly – keep at least an hour or, better yet, an hour and a half each day unbooked. This is time for you and for ad hoc meetings. Most people spend FAR too much time in 'routine' or 'pre-booked' formal meetings and have no time to work on what just came up that is important. (Lots of things that are **important** are not **urgent** – see rule 2.)

Make a list each day of the important things you are working on currently – put a star by the top-priority ones.

Cross off things as you get them done.

Before you go home at night, make a new list for the next day – rearrange priorities if necessary. Little things become big if left too long – unless they are not important anyway.

Seeing how you did with the old list at the end of the day, spending a few minutes looking at what remains on the list and planning the next day is time well spent.

If you have a driver or you commute on a train, during the day at the bottom of the same to-do sheet make a list of people you will call or text on the way home or on the way in tomorrow and what about – this uses time that would otherwise be wasted.

When you work at home, set a time limit – don't give yourself unlimited time. This will force you to make priorities and make you a better executive.

Rule 2 – LEARN HOW TO JUDGE PRIORITIES AND WHAT IS WORTH SPENDING TIME ON

	IMPORTANT	NOT IMPORTANT
URGENT (In your face!)	Everybody knows to work on these things!	Most people spend far too much time on these things!
NOT URGENT (No one is pushing you)	**Effective people make sure they carve out time for these things.**	Very few people spend time on these things

Learn the difference between **Important** and **Urgent**. Everyone works on Important and Urgent – hardly anyone works on Not Important and Not Urgent. The big mistake comes when people spend too much time on things that are urgent but not important and have no time left for things that are important but not urgent. This is the fundamental KEY to personal organisation. (Take the time to study *The 7 Habits of Highly Effective People* by Stephen R. Covey, https://www.stephencovey.com/7habits/7habits.php)

Rule 3 – MAKE OTHER PEOPLE DO THE WORK

I am going to take the space to include a politically incorrect American joke that was going around in the 1970s:

> *It happens in a large department store commercial office and one of the young attractive buyers came in to see the store CEO and said she was going to have to resign. She was a good buyer and she was in tears when she told him so he tenderly asked her why.*
>
> *She (unmarried) said she was pregnant. (In those days this was a problem!) She initially refused to tell him, but after his pushing her a bit, she told this story:*

She had been working late one night and the lights had gone out in the office and a man had come in and taken advantage of her. She then discovered several weeks later she was pregnant.

The store CEO was horrified and said, 'Who could possibly have done this thing?'

She replied, 'Oh, I know who did it – it was my commercial director!'

The CEO said, 'Wait a minute, if the lights were out and you could not see, how do you KNOW it was him?'

'That's easy,' the buyer said. 'He made me do all the work!'

It is an art form worth developing to learn to let your team do the work.

Don't do it for them – you have to teach them how and coach them, but THEY have to do it.

If you are home working and your team are out dancing you are a fool. They should have to do their jobs and a little bit of yours – that way they get ahead and you get ahead because the business gets ahead. If you do your job and a little bit of theirs, you go crazy and the business suffers.

When you are planning your priority list each day (see pages 172–3) ask yourself the questions:

- □   'Do I really have to do this?'
- □   'Does it really need to be done?'
- □   'Who else can I get to do it?'

The person who said *'If you want something done right, do it yourself'* doesn't know anything about running a big business. If you want something done right, have a good team, train and supervise them well, and teach them to do it! Then make sure they do!

Rule 4 – STORES ARE THE KEY TO COMMERCIAL SUCCESS

Most commercial people spend far too much of their time in the office – either doing things someone else can do or attending useless and boring meetings. (See more on meetings later.)

If you can, try to spend a day a week in the stores. I know this may sound impossible to you but it is not. If you cannot manage a day a week, then at least a day every two weeks is the minimum – as mentioned, half the time, go by yourself and half the time take one of your direct team with you. Half the time, tell the store you are coming and half the time just go. You will learn *a lot more* about your business in the stores than you do in the office! There are no customers in the office and the best information systems in the world are not a substitute for first-hand looking, talking and on-site information. Your team will reliably feed you with at least 150 per cent of the good news and only about 10 per cent of the bad. If you are in the stores one day a week you will know what is REALLY going on in your business.

In every business I have ever run I have worked hard to develop key relationships in the stores – I always had two or three really good department managers that were not afraid to talk to me and tell me what was going on. Do this and give them some time each week for store feedback. It will point you in the right direction for your priority list.

Once you develop the reputation as one who listens and respects stores, it will enhance your influence in the business.

Lastly, teach your category managers to do the same things I am advising you to do. They will all say they are 'too busy' but it's all about priorities. The more they understand what really happens at retail on the coal face, the more they will make good judgements when they are in the office or with a supplier. If you have a team member that does not get this plot, don't send them out alone: take them out with you until they get it!

So, why am I banging on about store visits in a chapter on organisation of your personal time?

In order to get the most out of your time, your decisions about actions and priorities have to be good ones – and going to the stores makes you more informed. It therefore makes you more able to set yourself the right personal priorities and the right priorities for your team.

One example might be a direct mailer that did not work – maybe the stock was not sufficient to back it?

Another example might be the loss of a key concession – you would probably pick that up on the first visit and be able to ask why and do something about it.

I suspect this will be hard to grasp if you don't already know it, but this major time investment will *save* you time, and you won't understand until you experience it for yourself.

If you don't believe anything else I tell you – believe this!

RULE 5 – YOU HAVE TO LEARN TO DO WHATEVER IS REQUIRED

Try to train yourself **and your team** not to think about 'their job' or 'their status' or 'their title' but what contribution they are making each hour and day to the success of the business. There might be a day when an assistant buyer does something more important than their boss or their boss's boss.

If you can build the spirit of everyone working together to 'do what needs doing' rather than people worrying about **'what is my job'** and **'what is someone else's job'** and, the most sinister of all, **'that's not my job!'**, you will get a lot more out of your team with the same time investment.

If you ask someone on your team to do something that needs doing and they reply 'that's not my job', then that person is someone you don't need on your team.

RULE 6 – DON'T WASTE TIME IN MEETINGS

Meetings are the biggest time-waster of all. Usually it is because no one has set the format or the structure or cares about wasting time. Let's take a weekly trade meeting, for example.

I have sat in on many meetings in which hours are spent poring over figures from various people when the meeting could have been done in ten minutes with a proper report. In a meeting like this everyone should have the same figures – prepared by whomever you designate and distributed ahead of time. The only comments should be to answer questions or explain something unusual in the figures. The rest of the time should be spent on specifics of the business – what is selling and why and what you are doing about getting more of the product; what is not selling and why and how you are going to get rid of it.

People spend hours babbling about 'this was up 21 per cent' and 'that was down 17 per cent' and it is a complete waste of time. Customers do not come into stores to buy percentages.

The percentages are only a reflection of actual product performance and the only thing that matters is the product and the performance and the reasons for it.

I sat through a dreadful trading meeting recently where hundreds of figures were discussed by a room full of people and I learned absolutely nothing about any product that was for sale or not, and nothing about what customers were buying or not – there was not one piece of product in the room or one bit of useful information passed!

You can get a *lot* more out of your meeting time by making sure the meeting focuses on the right things – don't give *any time* to recitation of meaningless and boring figures! Meetings should be alive and sparkling and involve talking about exciting things – usually something working for customers or not and what you are going to do to exploit the former and fix the latter. Nothing else matters.

Figures are the RESULT of running the business correctly, not the cause: you cannot run the business by figures. The figures are your report card at the end of term. The business is run by doing the work to have better product for customers in your stores.

RULE 7 – SPEND 99 PER CENT OF YOUR TIME LOOKING FORWARD

When you drive a car, you have to spend 99 per cent of your time looking out the windscreen to where you are going and only 1 per cent of your time looking in the rear-view mirror to see where you have been. If you spend too much time looking backwards, you might crash.

In order to get more from your time, only allow *very limited* forensics on where you have been and that is useful only as a guide to what you are going to do differently looking forward.

I learned a very valuable lesson from a colleague just a few years ago – NEVER DO A 'REVIEW' – ONLY MAKE NEW PLANS!

Looking forward is all that matters. There is a simple reason for this: neither you nor anyone else can change the past. It is gone – forever – it will never come again. The future, even tomorrow and the day after that, is always pretty uncertain. The only thing that really matters and where you can make a difference is today. What is everyone going to do TODAY that makes a difference for the future?

Yes, of course, be *guided* by the past but endless boring repeats of so-called analysis of 'what happened' are such a total and utter waste of time, I can hardly stay awake. All that matters is what we have learned and what we are now doing differently to make things better for customers.

RULE 8 – LEARN HOW TO RUN A 'RIGSBEE PILE'

Many years ago in Indianapolis when I was running L.S. Ayres & Co. for Associated Dry Goods, I worked with a colleague called Robert Rigsbee.

He had a pile of paper on his desk on the upper right-hand corner, which I wondered about every time I came to his office because the rest of his office, except for this pile of papers, was extremely tidy and organised.

I finally asked him about it one day and he told me his technique. Whenever someone sent him something he, like everyone else, binned the rubbish and dealt with the important stuff. However, this pile was for things of which he was not sure.

His technique was to put into this pile things that were not important enough to deal with now but not yet confirmed as rubbish for the bin.

Occasionally he had to refer back to something there because it turned out to be more important than he thought.

On the other hand, most of the issues went away and then, after a respectable time frame, he just pushed it off his desk and into the bin.

I started using this technique and it really works. In later years I learned that it works for emails as well.

It is really a form of 'triage':

1. Confirmed Rubbish – Bin it
2. Confirmed Important – Deal with it
3. Not Sure – Put it in the 'Rigsbee Pile'

You can learn a lot about people from learning about dogs.

I have owned dogs all my life. I was a trustee of the Battersea Dogs & Cats Home in London for 19 years, the last 11 as Vice Chairman and Chairman. Getting to know dogs and watching dogs has taught me a lot that applies to people as well.

BIG DOG BODY LANGUAGE

Big dogs don't 'attack' little dogs – they just ignore them. The language is 'I don't need to be bothered with the likes of you.' This is something to keep in mind when you are tempted to rise to a challenge from someone when it does not really matter. Save your energy and firepower for when it does matter.

MAKING THE DOG LIE DOWN

It is a strange but true fact that if you can make a dog adopt a passive position physically, this will be reflected in its mental attitude – the two are linked. If you can make the dog lie down, it will be more relaxed than if in a more 'ready' position.

I have found this same technique works with people. Sometimes in business, people have to work in a situation that they are not very happy about. If you can convince them to 'act happy' anyway, it has an amazing effect not only on them but on those around them and it really does make things better.

Try this on yourself first next time the occasion comes up –
you will then be ready to coach others on how to do it.

'The voluntary path to cheerfulness, if our spontaneous
cheerfulness be lost, is to sit up cheerfully, and act and
speak as if cheerfulness were already there. To feel brave,
act as if we were brave, use all our will to that end, and
courage will very likely replace fear. If we act as if from
some better feeling, the bad feeling soon folds its tent like an
Arab and silently steals away.'

William James, American philosopher

IGNORING BAD BEHAVIOUR

The best and most effective, and most kind, dog-training
techniques are to completely ignore bad behaviour and reward
good behaviour. It really works. This also works with people
as well. Save 'punishment' for some time when it really, really
matters (maybe never).

AND FINALLY

An old American proverb sometimes attributed to either Oliver
Wendell Holmes or Mark Twain:

'Even a dog knows the difference between being stumbled
over and being kicked.

If you intentionally harm someone, they will never forget it
. . . ever.'

Chapter 8

TIPS & TRUISMS

There is no substitute for experience and doing it yourself but it is possible to learn faster by paying attention to those who have done it successfully before.

There is a big difference between 'Supervision' and 'Management' and 'Leadership'.

Some people think that this has to do with the level you are at in the business hierarchy, i.e. lower-level 'supervisors', middle-level 'managers' and high-level 'leaders'.

My observations over a long time in the business is that the three types of behaviour patterns – all very different – of the people in charge operate at **all levels** of the business.

I have known 'supervisors' who were truly great leaders.

I have also, sadly, seen chief executives who were 'managers'.

Supervision involves direct contact and being responsible for what those on your team are doing, and usually when and how they are doing it.

Managers have a wider role in that this is the first level where they may be 'supervising' people who are in turn 'supervising' other people. This is the biggest jump you make in your business career because it calls for a whole new set of skills. You are no longer 'watching over' what people do all day but are setting up plans and objectives, and monitoring those plans and objectives. You also have an obligation to begin to influence policies set out by the company's 'leaders'.

Leadership is best defined by Sir John Hoskyns, who was the Chairman when I was CEO of the Burton Group: 'Leadership is a set of behaviours that invites and generates a following response.'

(Some sad people think 'leadership' is finding out what direction everyone is going and then jumping to the head of the queue!)

Leaders must, of course, have a good plan, reasonable budgets, good people in place – all the stuff that you learn in management training courses and books.

However, true leaders do something beyond this: they create an atmosphere that makes people want to get with the programme, do their best and have fun doing it. This is an art form that can be learned early on whatever job you have and, once you do learn it, you can go as far as you like.

The number of senior executives I have known who would personally rate themselves as good leaders is almost all. The ones who really were good leaders form a very small and exclusive group indeed.

Leadership is not a position or a title. It is a way of treating people in such a way that inspires them to do things right, do the right things, and inspires them to want to win.

The bigger the job
you have, the more
you can accomplish
just by asking the
right questions.

People are inveterate 'boss watchers'. They are interested in what the boss says and does, and which direction the 'wind is blowing' – so to speak!

You can use this to advantage by being very careful what you choose as a topic. The less you see of an individual or a group of individuals, the more critical it is that you PRIORITISE carefully what message you want to send.

It took me a long time to learn that people can only remember about three things – if you spout off tons of questions or comments or instructions, it is left to chance whether they will choose the one you really wanted them to act on.

Therefore, before you spend time with people in your organisation, whether it is a meeting with your top team, a store visit or just walking around the office, always take the time to think about the fact that whatever you say and whatever you do might be remembered, repeated and, yes, gossiped about.

This can be a more powerful communication tool than the 'Company Newsletter' or pages of 'instruction memos'.

We are all sending messages all the time – to our families, our friends, our colleagues and our customers. It is worth the time to think about what these messages will be. The bigger your job and the better you want to be at it, the more you will need to perfect this skill.

It is easy to know what is wrong – almost anyone who works in a business knows the things that are wrong. What is of **value** is knowing how to fix things.

Just being right about what's wrong is of very limited value. The world is full of people who can wax lyrical about what is wrong. They don't have to be very senior or very clever, really.

Having a realistic idea of what could be done or a plan to fix things is what creates lasting value in a business and this ability is all too rare.

This is a lesson you should first teach yourself and then teach to everyone who works for you.

'Moaners' deserve very little of your time. People who have a grasp of what needs to be done to make things better deserve a lot of your time and support.

People who know what is wrong and come to you with a plan to fix it should be considered for promotion!

Make it obvious to your team that what you really value are 'solutions' – not 'problems'.

MARGARET THATCHER'S TRICK:

When Maggie Thatcher was in her heyday as Prime Minister, I was lucky enough on one occasion at a drinks party to have a chat with her, one to one, and could not resist teasing her to tell me 'her best secret' – it was a good-humoured conversation and finally she said it was this:

'When I have a cabinet meeting and someone is having a long moan about something, at the end (or before the end if I get too impatient) I say: "What are you suggesting?"'

I have used this trick many times over the years and it usually works wonders. The look on their face makes your day!

Everyone knows that 'big things' are more important than 'little things'. However, not everyone knows what the big things are! This applies to mistakes, problems and opportunities.

MISTAKES

Mistakes are part of being human. Mistakes increase in direct proportion to the number of opportunities to make the mistake multiplied by how easy it is to make the mistake.

PROBLEMS

A small problem can become a big problem when it is repeated over and over and over and over or if it affects enough people often enough.

OPPORTUNITIES

A little opportunity can become a big opportunity if it is repeated over and over or if it has the chance to grow by itself or with a little help.

Around 1986 when I was running L.S. Ayres in Indiana and Associated Dry Goods had been taken over by May Company, I was doing a store tour with David Farrell, the Chief Executive of May Company, and a group of colleagues.

We were in the young men's department and he remarked that we were missing the number-one-selling style of 'Bugle Boy' trousers, which was the hot line of the moment.

I made the fatal mistake of saying to him, 'I cannot imagine how the CEO of the entire company could pay attention to that kind of little detail,' at which point he turned to me in front of the entire tour group and said: 'The reason I am CEO of the company and you are not is I know the difference between a big thing and a little thing!'

That humiliating reprimand stayed with me over the years and as I went on to run more and more stores I learned that problems and opportunities multiply: if you have a lot of stores or a lot of people working for you, when you get something right, you get it right over and over. When you get something wrong, you get it wrong over and over.

I learned in Tesco (whilst working as a cashier in a store!) that scanning our clothing bar codes required that the cashier used two hands because the ticket had to be turned over – we then printed the tickets differently (a small thing) so that they could be scanned with one hand. This 'tiny little thing' sped up thousands of transactions every week in hundreds of stores and is still making a difference every time a garment is scanned.

You should be getting the idea by now.

Retail is a business where you can never get it 100 per cent right – you can only make it better and better!

If you are a person who requires perfection, you should not be in the retail business.

The factors that prevent you getting things 100 per cent right – ever – are:

- ☐ Your customers
- ☐ Your suppliers
- ☐ Your competitors
- ☐ Your government
- ☐ Your business environment and the economic cycle
- ☐ The weather
- ☐ Developing news – e.g. health scares, a horsemeat scandal, inflammable kids' clothes

Your customers keep changing – they not only change individually and by group in their wants and needs, but you are also constantly losing old customers and gaining new ones. Because this group change is so dynamic, you can never have a 100 per cent perfect offer.

Your suppliers have business problems just like you do – even if you give them all the 100 per cent right instructions, it does not always turn out that way.

Your competitors are not standing still. They are planning to get better, just like you are, and most of them will improve or they won't be around very long. They also keep you from getting it 100 per cent right.

Your government will continue to change the rules of engagement from time to time, with rules about staff, rules about customers, rules about taxes, etc. As the rules change, you have to change and you have to stay ahead of it.

The general business environment also changes. The economic cycle goes up and down. Clothing trends and spend trends go up and down.

I am not saying 'relax and let it all happen' – far from it – I am just suggesting that you have to go into each season knowing no matter how well you think you have it planned and executed, lots of things will turn out in retrospect to have been wrong.

Don't spend time agonising – just make plans to make it all better.

Finally, current press campaigns can spring out of nowhere – and the press always love a scare story. You have to expect the unexpected!

'Fifty-four per cent of all statistics are made up!'

'The devil is in the detail.'

In order to get the right answers, you have to ask the right questions!

An understanding of how to read and interpret what the figures are telling you is an essential part of running a retail business whether you are a store manager, a buyer, a commercial director or a CEO.

The first thing is to be sure that what you are reacting to is accurate. When I say 54 per cent of all statistics are made up, I have no way of proving that but you have no way of proving it is not true either. Over the years I have found that a lot of what is presented, sometimes in elaborate form, is completely misleading if not downright untrue.

The most common mistake is raising the point of contact with the truth to such a distant vantage point that it all becomes homogenised.

Example: 5 per cent staff absence sounds pretty good until you find out that it is only 2 per cent during weekdays, when more reliable people are working, but 14 per cent on Saturday morning when you need the staff most and some of them have been out drinking the night before and can't be bothered to come to work.

Example: 1.5 per cent of stock loss in clothing sounds under control until you realise that this is made up of a bunch of stock 'overages' in some stores (which cannot possibly be accurate) and losses in some other stores of up to 10 per cent.

Example: 20 per cent of staff turnover sounds difficult but manageable until you learn that it is made up from less than 5 per cent in stable areas and up to 40 per cent in problem areas.

Example: that we are 95 per cent in stock at all times sounds almost OK until we learn that we are 5 per cent out of stock at all times. Also this could be 2 per cent out of stock in many areas and 10 per cent out of stock in hard-to-manage areas, which means you are disappointing one out of every ten customers!

When I lost my baggage once in St Louis after a long flight and faced my visit with no change of clothes, the airline (TWA, now bankrupt) told me proudly that '98 per cent of all bags get through with no problem'.

Would you fly on an airline where 98 per cent of the flights got through without crashing? (Sorry about the 2 per cent!)

How about this more accurate communication? 'Before you fly with us, please remember that we lose 2 out of every 100 bags we handle so be sure to have a change of underwear and a toothbrush in your hand luggage!'

It is amazing how many times I see reports that say 'we do 7 per cent of our business in this store and 5 per cent of our business in that store'. Accurate, probably; meaningful, not at all in any sense that you can do anything constructive with it.

What you want to know is 'How much of the store's business do you do? By store? What are the factors where the penetration is high? If you can do 10 per cent of the store's business in some stores, what is wrong in the stores where your participation is only 5 per cent?'

Every time you look at figures ask yourself, 'What can or should I do about this?' If the answer is nothing, you are looking at the wrong figures!

How to know if something is worth doing or not:

☐   Is it in line with your overall goals?

☐   Is it really possible to do – have you got the capability, the time, the money?

☐   Will it really make a difference?

☐   Are the results worth the effort?

It is possible
for several
independent 'good'
decisions to come
together in such a
way that the overall
outcome for the
business is 'bad'.

I first discovered this about 40 years ago and at that time called it 'The Department Store Syndrome' because I mistakenly thought it was endemic to department stores.

I soon learned that it is universal to human nature and any business where there is more than one person making the decisions.

The bigger the company, the more likely this situation is to occur.

If you are the person in charge, you have to realise that a problem may not necessarily be caused by any one decision or action – even though it may appear so. It might be caused by a combination of decisions.

Just as in chemistry, when you mix two apparently harmless chemicals you can get an explosion. Two or more apparently harmless (or even good) ideas can mix together in a way that does not give a good outcome for the business.

This is never more prevalent than in decisions made by the 'buying office' when mixed with decisions made by 'the stores'. This is one of the reasons I am so enthusiastic about the importance of bringing these two sides of the organisation together.

You then mix in decisions made by the finance department in line with their priorities, and by the logistics department in line with their priorities, and you can begin to see how the situation can develop.

This is why looking for a way to 'apportion blame' is a mug's game. Just look for solutions going forward.

Many times in life and in business you don't have the luxury of selecting a 'good' option – sometimes you have to select the 'least bad' option!

Would it not be wonderful if the world was an orderly place and everything was fair and rational?

Alas, this is not to be and because you are dealing all the time with human beings plus a series of random events, many of which cannot be explained rationally, sometimes you get into a situation where, when you examine all your options, you just can't seem to find a 'good' one that gives you the outcome you would like.

In this situation, you have to face up to it and forget trying to find a 'good option' and begin to accept that the best outcome is the 'least bad' option.

This happens a lot more than you might imagine and if you have not yet found yourself in this situation, you will.

There is no point in elaborate examples – there are no rules for this situation, but you will recognise it when you are in it!

'Sleeping on it'
is not just an old
wives' tale – it can
really be a way to
make you more
effective.

A group of Dutch scientists conducted studies over ten years that confirmed a theory that it's easier for the brain to process complex information when it's sleeping. Their theory was published in 2006. The research is still ongoing and some scientists disagree.

However, I have always found personally that 'sleeping' on things really does improve my thinking process. Walking the dogs also sometimes works the same way.

It really works for me to think hard about something – write down the pros and cons, form some initial thoughts – and then let it go. Don't try to make a decision right away.

If you can, literally 'sleep on it' and, by the next day, your brain may have sorted out some of the less obvious bits and pieces that go into a good decision.

In addition to using your subconscious mind to sort out little details, it creates time and distance for you to be objective about the problem.

This works for you alone or with decision-making groups. Sometimes a quick decision is required, but if it is not, sleep on it!

'Anyone who has never made a mistake has never tried anything new.'

Albert Einstein

'We know how to pursue and how to flee with the same swiftness.'

Parthian message to Alexander the Great. The Parthian Empire lasted from 250 BC to around AD 220. They developed the technique of shooting backwards as they retreated – hence the 'Parthian shot' (now sometimes called the 'parting shot').

Knowing when to quit is an essential skill for a successful gambler. It is also important for a business as well.

I quoted my old friend Joe Noble earlier that 'Everyone has the right to make mistakes – they don't have the right to procrastinate about fixing them.'

Of all the things you have to learn in retailing, one of the most important is to learn when to quit. This applies to buyers and the products they bought (which they tend to be in love with) all the way up to programmes beloved by the chief executive.

Retailing is about trying things to see what works. If it works, do more. If it does not work, stop it and try something else.

I could fill this entire book with agonising stories about projects that were always going to fail and went on far too long.

However, I could fill another book with stories of projects that appeared to be too difficult to do at first and were successful in the end.

Knowing when to 'press on' and when to 'cut and run' is one of the most important aspects of successful retailing. The problem is . . . I can't give you a formula for knowing when to do what.

What I can do is tell you that you should be asking yourself all the time which situation you are most likely to be dealing with and make your plans accordingly.

Self-confidence and self-doubt are **not** mutually exclusive!

Slick perfection of presentation is the enemy of spirited and open feedback – learn how to use 'rough drafts' instead.

It is a waste of your time and, in fact, counterproductive to the desired result to have things in 'perfect' form before you ask others to contribute their ideas.

The more 'slick' the format, the less likely it will be that people will feel comfortable giving you feedback.

Just the simple act of CALLING it a 'draft' works wonders.

If you have a polished finished product and say, 'I would like to get your feedback,' you are saying the words but the appearance of the product defies anyone to say anything other than 'great stuff'. (This especially applies when you are the boss!)

Bang out your draft and use that – warts and all – to solicit feedback. It will even help you to form a different attitude in your own mind to the feedback.

If you have spent hours perfecting something, it becomes yours – body and soul – and it makes it harder to be open to criticism or suggestions, however valid.

Try this trick next time you are writing a paper or a presentation and want some input from your colleagues or your team.

Look at it another way:

A girl spends two hours getting ready for a party and then just before she is ready to go out the door, asks her partner, 'How do I look?' (There is only one possible answer!)

- To look is one thing.

- To see what you are looking at is another.

- To understand what you are seeing is a third.

- To learn from what you understand is still something else.

- But to ACT on what you learned is all that really matters!

Four things I have learned from flying:

Being a pilot has taught me a lot, including these four points which are explored throughout this chapter. When it is your life and the lives of others for which you are responsible, it clears the mind. I also learned about learning – what helped me to learn and what just frustrated me.

- ☐ **Direction is more important than speed.** If you are going the right direction, you will get there, no matter what the speed. If you are going in the wrong direction you will never get there, no matter how fast you are going.

- ☐ **No matter how many times a pilot has taken off in the airplane, they always go through the checklist.** If it matters, have a checklist!

- ☐ **You learn best when you are having fun**. Joy increases the ability to learn. Stress hampers the ability to learn.

- ☐ **In order to be good, you sometimes have to be able to do two things at once.**

Direction is
more important
than speed and
how you **deal**
with the two is
exactly **opposite**.
Direction correction
must be instant.
You can afford
to wait longer for
speed.

Flying has taught me a lot about leadership. If you are heading from London to Paris and you fly at 170 degrees you will get there – in a jet or in a Tiger Moth. However, if you fly at 190 degrees you will NEVER get to Paris and will probably end up in Barcelona.

The same analogy holds true to managing and leading the members of your team. If they are headed in the right direction, but going a little slower than you might have liked, encourage them, help them and support them. They will eventually gain speed and you will have a solid performance.

On the other hand, if any member of the team is going in a **direction** that is different from the one you have agreed with the team, this is not only disruptive to other members of the team but will waste their efforts. You must, in this case, take corrective action immediately.

There is another problem with directional errors – just as is true in flying – the longer they go on, the more difficult it is to correct them. If you have been flying the wrong way for a minute, you can correct back to course in a minute. If you have been flying the wrong way for an hour, it might take 90 minutes to correct.

One of the most important aspects of leadership is to be absolutely certain that the team is all pulling in the same direction.

Anything short of this causes trouble and wastes effort.

When you are under pressure, your IQ goes down by 25 per cent. Have your 'disaster drills' memorised.

All pilots are trained on what to do in the event of a fire or an engine failure. This is not theoretical training; it is a list of MEMORISED ACTIONS that are to be done immediately.

By the time a disaster happens, it is too late to figure out what you are going to do – you need to know what you are going to do in advance.

A good example of a disaster drill is the threat of losing a good employee.

You should have a rule with all your direct team that if any of their own team should resign, you need to know about it WITHOUT DELAY.

The theory of this is that all people are important – if they are not, they should not be in their jobs anyway. Therefore, if a good person wants to leave for any reason, that is important and you should know ahead of time what you are going to do.

I have saved a lot of good people over my career by knowing about it soon enough and moving into action quickly enough.

You would be surprised how many people don't consider doing this and just react to someone leaving with sadness and a sense of inevitability.

There will be other situations where you need to know ahead of time what you are going to do without having to come up with a scheme.

These might include:

- A serious accident or death on the job
- One of your locations coming under attack or being destroyed by fire or flood
- Discovery of a fraud
- Potential take-over bid for the company
- Loss of a key supplier
- A major systems outage

Make your own list and memorise your disaster drills. And, make sure your team can identify a disaster when one strikes!

Some other things I have learned:

- ☐ It is true that forgiveness is often easier to obtain than permission, but when you employ this technique you'd better be right because you take all the risk!
- ☐ The boss gets 150 per cent of the good news and only about 10 per cent of the bad news. React to the bad as a sample of things you might not have heard about.
- ☐ Retailing is a business that teaches you the difference between simple and easy.
- ☐ The only way to eat a whale is a bite at a time.
- ☐ There are limits to human intelligence but there are no limits to human stupidity.
- ☐ If you don't know where you are going, any road will get you there.
- ☐ It's not what you do that matters; it's what you get DONE!
- ☐ Sometimes people have to support the boss even though they think he is wrong. It works the other way round as well.
- ☐ It is hard to eat like a bird and poop like an elephant!
- ☐ Ready! Fire! Aim! – Whoops!
- ☐ It's better to be rich and healthy than to be poor and unwell. Don't accept 'trade-offs' unless you have to.
- ☐ No amount of planning replaces dumb luck!
- ☐ Averages can be misleading. On average, the bigger group or cluster they apply to, the more likely they are to be misleading.
- ☐ The closest correlation of any internal number to the overall profitability of the business is margin per square foot (or metre).

- ☐ Sitting around theorising when the facts are available is a complete and utter, and even dangerous, waste of time.
- ☐ In a workshop, never let the presentations take up any more than ONE HALF the time. This keeps the presentations carefully edited and generates good discussions. Don't let them run over either! People get tired of being 'talked at'.
- ☐ Never put all your eggs in one basket, supplier wise – always have at least two viable suppliers in any important category.

Reading list of books that have helped me a lot:

- ☐ *The 7 Habits of Highly Effective People* – Stephen R. Covey
- ☐ *The Learning Revolution* – Gordon Dryden
- ☐ *The World Is Flat* – Thomas L. Friedman
- ☐ *What the Animals Tell Me* – Beatrice Lydecker
- ☐ *The Popcorn Report: Faith Popcorn on the Future of Your Company, Your World, Your Life* – Faith Popcorn
- ☐ *Gourmet Magazine Cookbooks*, Volumes 1 and 2
- ☐ *The Tipping Point: How Little Things Can Make a Big Difference* – Malcolm Gladwell
- ☐ *The Black Swan: The Impact of the Highly Improbable* – Nassim Nicholas Taleb

POSTSCRIPT

There are literally millions of retail outlets all over the world, from one-person shops to giant hypermarkets and giant department stores.

My purpose in writing this book was to make the things I have learned throughout my 56 years in the business available to anyone who might find them helpful – maybe they will help someone to avoid one of the many hundreds of mistakes I made in the learning process.

This book is aimed at everyone who is interested in retail but a lot of it applies to any business.

I have had a lot of fun learning all this and I have had a lot of fun writing it all down as well. If you have not had fun reading it, then I have failed!

John Hoerner

Appendix

SOME OF MY FAVOURITE RECIPES

RECIPES

I hope you enjoyed the retailing recipes. Following are some of my favourite ones for the kitchen – just like my retailing recipes, they are not exact prescriptions but a general idea of what works. You will have to contribute your own techniques to make them great. At the end, I will tell you one more way that retailing recipes are like cooking recipes.

GRANDMA STONE'S CHICKEN SOUP

This serves 4–6 people.

Get a large stockpot.
- ☐ Put in a chicken – Tesco organic free-range is the best
- ☐ 1 onion
- ☐ 1 leek
- ☐ 1 carrot
- ☐ 1 bay leaf, some thyme and whatever other herbs you like
- ☐ 2 cloves
- ☐ 10 peppercorns
- ☐ Stalk of celery **including the leaves** – as many leaves as you have

Cook until boiling on the AGA boiling plate or high heat on your hob. Then put in the AGA simmer oven or in a low oven (temp 95°C) and leave just under boiling for as long as possible – overnight is best but if you start in the morning it can be ready for dinner.

While the soup is simmering, make the noodles:
- ☐ 6 egg yolks
- ☐ 1 whole egg
- ☐ 1 tsp of salt
- ☐ Beat the above

Put as much flour into the egg mixture as it will take. Fork first and then sift and knead on a floured board or countertop.

Roll it out *as thin as you can* with a rolling pin. Then roll it up into a tight scroll and slice into narrow strips. Shake the noodles out and leave to dry on a kitchen towel in a warm, dry (but not hot) place.

When the soup is done, take out and bone the chicken. Throw away the original vegetables.

Reserve the best parts of the chicken meat – give the rest to the dogs.

Let the broth stand to cool and then skim. Strain the broth through a fine sieve.

Then start over with the broth with new vegetables to taste – carrot, onion, leek, celery . . . I sometimes throw in only one handful of rice to slightly thicken the broth. When the vegetables are almost done, add in the noodles. When the noodles are almost done (this does not take long with fresh pasta) put in the chicken at the last minute. (If you boil the chicken too long it will shred up because it is so cooked.)

This soup is not only delicious but is thought by some to cure a cold!

KILLER SALAD DRESSING

This recipe makes a jam jar's worth of dressing. Crush 2–3 cloves of fresh garlic depending on size. Chopping is no good; it needs to be crushed in a garlic crusher.

Use a medium-size jar with a tight lid (275ml). I love the Bonne Maman-style jam jars for this.

Put the garlic in the jar. Add 2 level teaspoons of honey. Add 4 tablespoons or more of strong Dijon mustard, the kind with plenty of kick to it.

Mix the mustard, honey and garlic. Then add about a scant teaspoon of salt, 20–30 grinds of fresh pepper, and a teaspoon each of dried dill, basil, tarragon (generous), thyme and oregano (less or more according to taste).

Mix up well in the bottom of the jar.

You now have all the flavouring present so it is time to add the oil and vinegar. I use olive oil and a ratio of at least 3½:1 or 4:1 oil to vinegar.

I use **5 kinds of vinegar**: cider, white wine, red wine, balsamic and sherry. Put the oil in first, then fill up with the vinegars – using each kind to your own taste.

Now stir all the ingredients together using a fork or whisk – then shake the jar vigorously. (If you have a self-winding watch take it off before you shake because I do mean vigorously!) If required, you can use the dressing right away, but it is much better if you have made it ahead of time and kept it in the refrigerator because it has more flavour after a couple of days. When you do that, take it out of the refrigerator an hour before you intend to use it, and then give it a big shake again before dressing your salad.

If this turns out to be too strong for you, cut down on the garlic and the mustard.

This saves beautifully – easily for a week or two and possibly up to a month or more.

SUE ROBERTS'S CHICKEN

Roast a free-range organic chicken – or the best chicken you can find. Cook on the well-done side (see recipe for 'Roast Chicken' on page 240).

The night before take the meat apart by hand. Give the skin and all grisly bits to the dogs. Arrange the hand-separated (not cut up) pieces in a flat porcelain dish.

Marinate in 'Killer Salad Dressing'. However, cut down on the vinegar by half and substitute lemon juice – also keep the garlic to a minimum. It's a good idea to shift around the chicken the next morning to be sure the marinade coats every piece well. You should have used the right amount of marinade so there are no runny leftovers in the bottom of the dish.

About an hour before you are ready to serve, stir in a container of crème fraîche – one container per chicken. Coat all pieces well, mixing the crème fraîche with the marinade. Cover with halved green grapes and either parsley or salad cress for appearance.

Serve cold.

EGGS

If you fancy trying an American favourite called 'eggs over easy' here is the perfect method.

Use a small frying pan – non-stick or stainless steel with slanted sides is best. Put in a small amount of butter and cook the eggs just like you would do for 'sunny side up' and then, at the last minute, **remove the pan from the heat**, flip the eggs over and count to ten. Then take them out.

Removing the pan from the heat cools it down a little and ten seconds is just right to get the tops done but not overcook the yolks.

For perfect boiled eggs, try Albert Roux's recipe:

Start with as many eggs as you like in a pan of *cold* water. Bring the eggs to the boil (the more eggs, the longer it will take) and, once the water is boiling merrily, take the eggs out. For very soft eggs, take out right away; if you like them more done, you can wait 30 seconds or up to 60 seconds after the boil. Remember the eggs are cooking slowly while the water is coming up to the boil so be ready to take them out right away or they will get too done.

MEAT LOAF (serves 6)

This is my adjusted version based on Helen Corbitt's meatloaf in the *Nieman Marcus Cookbook* published in 1957.

Mix together:
- [ ] 2lbs lean beef mince
- [ ] 4oz pork belly, chopped fine
- [ ] 1 cup (240ml) breadcrumbs (soft is fine)
- [ ] 2 tbsp onion, chopped fine

Mix separately:
- [ ] 2 eggs
- [ ] 1 cup milk
- [ ] 3 tbsp melted butter
- [ ] 1 tbsp prepared horseradish
- [ ] 3 tbsp ketchup
- [ ] Approximately ¼ tsp of pepper to taste
- [ ] 2 tsp salt

Have ready:
- [ ] 3 thinly sliced strips of bacon

Mix dry ingredients (mince, pork belly, breadcrumbs, onion) thoroughly.

Mix eggs, milk, melted butter, horseradish, ketchup and seasoning in a separate bowl. Add the liquid to the dry ingredients slowly and work it all in together thoroughly. I use my hands for this.

Butter a loaf tin (approximately 4 x 8 inches) and pack the mixture in tightly. Arrange the strips of bacon on the top.

Cook in a moderate oven (170–190°C) for at least 90 minutes – I think 2 hours is better as you get more flavour when it is really well done.

This is good hot with baked, au gratin or scalloped potatoes, and the leftovers are also good cold in sandwiches with lettuce and mayonnaise.

BLOODY GOOD BLOODY MARY MIX

In a 2-litre jug, mix together:
- ☐ 1 litre of tomato juice
- ☐ Juice of 1 lemon*
- ☐ 2 tsp of caster sugar
- ☐ 1 tsp of salt
- ☐ 15 or 20 grinds of pepper
- ☐ 1 tbsp or more of **prepared horseradish sauce** (Tesco's Finest or Coleman's works well)
- ☐ 6–8 shakes of Tabasco sauce
- ☐ 10+ generous shakes of Worcestershire sauce
- ☐ 2 or 3 shakes of **soy sauce** – maybe 1 tbsp in all
- ☐ About 1 tsp of celery salt
- ☐ A generous squeeze of OXO liquid beef stock mix or 1 or 2 OXO cubes

---

* The following is optional but I think it matters in the taste: when I finish squeezing the lemon I make sure all the pips are out and then cut the rind into six pieces – I then put it into the mix and bang it around with the whisk and, finally, pour the mixture through the rinds in the funnel when putting it into the bottle.

Stir this up with a whisk until thoroughly mixed. Let it sit for an hour or two before bottling up.

I save this in a re-used whisky bottle and keep it in the fridge for several days. I always think that, like a lot of things, it gets better on the second day. It will keep for at least a week.

Serve cold, stirred with ice, and poured into a glass containing vodka according to your own taste – it stands up to as much as you want to put in or is good as a 'Virgin Mary' or 'Bloody Shame' on its own.

HAVE YOU EVER TRIED A 'BLOODY BEER'?
Don't knock it if you haven't tried it!
Fill a glass with ice, pour in equal parts lager and Bloody Mary, mix and stir. Prepare to be surprised!

FAKED BEANS

These are not nearly as good as the 'Baked Beans' later in the recipe section but they are very good and take a lot less time.

Serves 4 nicely – it can easily be doubled; add 5 minutes to each baking time.

In a bowl mix:
- [ ] 1 can of Heinz Baked Beans
- [ ] 1 can of drained haricot or flageolet beans
- [ ] 1 tbsp of dark brown sugar
- [ ] 1½ tbsp of dark treacle or blackstrap molasses
- [ ] 1 tbsp of mustard
- [ ] 2 tbsp of ketchup
- [ ] Half or less of a small onion chopped very fine
- [ ] 1–2 slices of smoked streaky bacon cut up into very fine chunks with scissors

Mix this all together and put in a baking dish (one where the mixture ends up 2–3 inches deep is ideal for short time preparation). When I have time, I cook for an hour in the AGA bake oven (160°C) covered with a lid or foil and 30 minutes in the AGA roasting oven (175°C) uncovered.

SUE'S CUCUMBERS

Do this the night before:

Start with 1 or 2 cucumbers depending on how many people you want to serve.

Select a bowl that has a lid or one that you can cover with cling film.

Start slicing the cucumbers and make a full layer in the bottom of the bowl. Then add a layer of thin-sliced raw onion rings. Alternate layers until the bowl is full.

Pour over brine solution to cover it all. (Brine is 2 tablespoons of salt to 500ml of water, approximately.)

Cover the dish with a lid or cling film and put in the refrigerator.

The next morning, pour out a third of the brine and substitute with vinegar – white, malt, wine, it does not matter (I sometimes use half white and half malt).

Cover the dish again and put back in the fridge.

It will be ready to serve by lunchtime and even better by dinnertime.

That's it!

PS Some people eat the onions as well!

SALAD CROUTONS

Take 2–3 slices of white or brown bread or toast. Cut off the crusts and cut the bread into squares about 1 inch (2.5cm) square.

Put equal parts butter and olive oil into a frying pan to cover the bottom generously. Add crushed or finely chopped garlic, dried oregano, dried thyme, generous salt and scant pepper to taste.

Fry the croutons on one side until golden (be careful not to burn them) and then turn over, pushing them around. If they have absorbed all the butter and olive oil, add a little more.

Fry them on the second side and then remove to a square of kitchen roll to drain and cool.

Great in any salad.

This is a recipe that takes a few times to get just right according to your own taste. You can adjust all the ingredients to get exactly the right balance for you.

JOHN'S RICH SPAGHETTI BOLOGNESE (serves 6)

Dice 1 small onion and 1 shallot. Chop 2 decent-size pieces of garlic. Put in a deep skillet or iron roasting dish and cover with a generous amount of olive oil. Season with oregano and basil (about a teaspoon of each). Cook until the onions are clear. Take out and set aside.

In the same skillet start browning 1 kg (2.2lbs) of mince. The better the mince, the better the sauce will be. Use fairly high heat because you want the meat to brown as well as cook.

While the meat is cooking, chop 3 stalks of celery and **a half-bottle of green olives**. Chop 1 green pepper (red is OK but green is better). Chop up about 6 medium-size mushroom caps. Reserve all this with the onions.

When the meat is thoroughly brown, cooked all the way through and starting to stick and be crusty on the pan, put in 2 cans of chopped tomatoes. (Save the cans.) Then put in a jar of Original Dolmio sauce. Just let it sit for a minute.

Half fill the Dolmio jar with red wine. Shake to clean the jar. Pour into the first empty tomato can and stir to clean the sides, then pour into the second can and stir. Then dump into the skillet.

Stir the red sauce around, then add a third to a half of a tube of tomato paste. Stir again. Then add all the reserved ingredients, i.e. chopped onions, shallot, garlic, olive, celery, mushrooms and pepper.

Stir carefully and well, and then cook over low heat or in a simmer oven for at least an hour. Two hours is better.

I always make plenty of sauce and plenty of spaghetti for good leftovers for the freezer:

Use scissors to cut up leftover spaghetti; mix in leftover sauce. Put it all into an oven-and-freezer-proof baking dish greased with butter or olive oil. Cover the top with grated sharp Cheddar cheese and grated Parmesan. Cover with cling film, then cover with aluminium foil and freeze. This can be taken from the freezer and put directly into a moderate oven to thaw for about an hour to 90 minutes.

GOOD OLD AMERICAN CHILLI

This recipe will serve 4–6 but I always make this amount even for two as it freezes beautifully.

Cut up 1 medium-size onion, 1 shallot (if you don't have a shallot use 2 onions), and 2–3 garlic cloves depending on size. Cut up 1 green pepper into tiny pieces. (If you don't have green, red will do.) Put all this in a large frying pan with olive oil, a generous sprinkling of dried oregano (2–3 teaspoons), 2 teaspoons of salt and about 20 grinds of ground pepper. Sauté this until the onions are clear, remove to a plate and reserve.

Now take 1kg (2.2lbs) of lean steak mince. (You can use regular mince but it will be a bit greasy.) Put half of this in the frying pan you used to cook the onions and the other half in the bottom of a 3-litre or larger metal pot with a lid. Now brown the mince carefully and well. Break into tiny pieces as it cooks and be sure that you get it really brown – if you get some brown stuck to the pan, you are doing it right. This is what makes the rich flavour.

When the meat is thoroughly brown, put it all in the big pot. Use a little red wine to deglaze the frying pan and put that in the big pot as well. Now add 2 cans of chopped tomatoes and 3 cans of beans. I use 2 cans of red kidney beans and 1 can of haricot or cannellini beans. All the beans should be drained and washed in a colander or sieve.

Half fill an empty tomato can with red wine and stir, then pour into the other can and stir, then pour into the chilli. Stir in the reserved Vegatables and squeeze in about a third of a tube of tomato paste. Add 2 dried bay leaves and **2 or 3 cloves, ground or smashed fine**.

The matter of chilli powder is down to personal taste – I use mild and don't use very much. Other people like hot chilli powder and lots of it. My suggestion is to start with 1 or 2 teaspoons of mild and take it from there according to your taste preference.

Now add between 500ml and 1 litre of tomato juice. I use a full litre because I prefer chilli to be like soup in a bowl. Serve with grated sharp Cheddar on rice cakes (put in the hot oven for 5 minutes). If you are really decadent or ravenous, it is great with grilled cheese sandwiches. On the other hand, if you like your chilli served over rice, then use less tomato juice, just enough to make it the right consistency.

In my opinion the chilli is best cooked for 2 hours or more (covered and slowly simmering) before serving. Some people say it is even better warmed on the second day!

PARSNIP CHIPS

Wash the parsnips and remove the heads and long tails. Do not peel!

Cut in half lengthwise. Split the narrow (bottom) end into 4 slices, cut the fat (top) end into 4 slices, then divide again into 8 slices.

If using right away, you can skip the next step.

If not using right away, put the cut strips into enough water to cover. Dry thoroughly before using.

Spray a small roasting pan with non-stick cooking spray. Then use just enough sunflower oil to cover each parsnip piece so they won't stick – 1 tablespoon per parsnip is plenty for this.

Toss the parsnip chips in the sunflower oil in the roasting pan and then put in the hot oven for 20 minutes. (The hot oven is AGA upper right, or set the oven for 200°C.)

After 20 minutes, take out and turn so they brown on two sides.

Roast for another 15 minutes.

If you have done this right they should not be greasy and should be delicious as a vegetable or as a potato substitute.

By not peeling and leaving the 'wood' intact in the centre, the parsnips are also high in fibre.

CHICKEN LIVER PÂTÉ

The recipe for 1 batch serves 4 as a lunch course, 6 for a first course or 8 with drinks. When I make it for a drinks party I do 3 batches, which fill two 500ml crocks to the top. This is enough for 25 or 30 people assuming you have other snacks as well.

Ingredients	For 3 batches	For 2 batches	For 1 batch
225g pack of frozen chicken livers – I use Tesco Easy Cook	3	2	1
Spring onions	6	4	2
Cognac	10 tbsp	7 tbsp	4 tbsp
Dry mustard	6 tsp	4 tsp	2 tsp
Mace powder	¾ tsp	½ tsp	¼ tsp
Dried thyme (increase if using fresh)	3 tsp	2 tsp	1 tsp
Medium to big cloves garlic	6	4	2
*Butter to fry herbs and livers	75g	50g	25g
*Butter for pâté	450g	300g	150g
*Butter to pour over top	150g	100g	50g
Total unsalted butter	675g	450g	225g
Dried bay leaf	1	1	1
Salt	3 tsp	2 tsp	1 tsp

The following directions are for 1 batch:

☐ Peel off the outer layer of the spring onions, split and chop very finely. Include some of the green tops.
☐ Peel and crush the garlic cloves.
☐ Put the onions and garlic in the frying pan with thyme and 25g of the butter. I like to put in a bay leaf as well and discard it later. Stir-fry the onions and garlic, thyme and bay leaf for 3 or 4 minutes only.

- ☐ Then add 225g of chicken livers – *well-thawed* and cut up in fairly fine chunks.
- ☐ Sauté the livers with the garlic and onions, thyme and bay leaf for about 6–7 minutes until they are cooked – turn them frequently.
- ☐ Unless your processor is pretty big, you will probably have to do this next part in 2 lots if you are doing enough for 3 batches!
- ☐ Discard the bay leaf and put the cooked liver, thyme, onions and garlic into a food processor.
- ☐ Put 2 tbsp of **cognac** into the cooling frying pan to get all the good flavour out and put that mixture with the rest of the cognac into the blender.
- ☐ Add the mustard, mace, and salt and pepper to taste. I use 1 tsp of salt and about 10–15 pepper grinds per 225g batch.
- ☐ Melt 150g of butter and pour over the mixture.
- ☐ Blend until you have a smooth pâté and put into a crock for drinks parties or individual dishes for lunch servings. Blend the mixture at least 3–4 times longer than you think you should for a smooth parfait (up to 10 minutes including some stops and starts or pulsing!).
- ☐ Melt the remaining 50g of the butter and pour over the top. I put a basil leaf on the top for presentation and it also helps to pour the butter on the basil leaf so it flows out evenly over the top of the pâté.
- ☐ Cover with cling film and chill in the bottom of the fridge for 24 hours minimum; 48 to 72 hours is better to bring out the most flavour before serving.

Serve with toast triangles and small sweet gherkins, and garnish with rocket or watercress.

---

*Tip to measure the butter easily: divide a 225g pack into thirds by eye and score – each third is 75g. Then divide one of the thirds again in three – each section is 25g.

HEALTHY SAUCE FOR FISH (serves 6)

- ☐ About 500g of cottage cheese – I use Tesco Low Fat
- ☐ About 1 cup (240ml) of yoghurt – I use Yeo Organic Vanilla
- ☐ About 1 tbsp (heaped) of Dijon (fairly hot) mustard
- ☐ **About half a small leek** – cut up finely
- ☐ 1–2 tsp of dill
- ☐ Salt
- ☐ Pepper

As you can see, this is all 'to taste' and it does not seem to matter very much about getting the proportions exactly right. You might like it with a little mayonnaise stirred in.

Mix thoroughly and serve.

To serve with fish, I find the sauce is better at room temperature rather than too cold so take it out of the fridge an hour ahead of time if you have made it earlier.

Healthy fish to go with the sauce:

Coat pan with sunflower oil.

Put sliced garlic on fish.

Put about 1 tsp of organic cider vinegar on each piece.

Bake in hot oven (AGA upper right or set the oven for 200°C): 20 minutes for normal; 40 minutes for very well done.

If it is salmon, sprinkle with a little dill.

SMOKED MACKEREL PÂTÉ
(serves 4 for first course – 8 for drinks)

The New Inn in Manaccan, Cornwall, has the most amazing smoked mackerel pâté. I was remarking on this while enjoying some there one day when a friendly lady at the next table piped up that hers was 'better' and she then proceeded to give me the recipe. You know what? It was better!

Tesco has great smoked mackerel – I take all the skin off and give it to the dogs but if you like your pâté rough you can leave it on!

First make a mixture of the soft stuff:
Start with a 300g tub of (not light!) cream cheese, and then blend in:
- □ 1–2 tbsp (heaped) mayonnaise (to taste)
- □ 1 tbsp sour cream
- □ Lemon juice (half a small lemon is enough – go easy on this, you can add more later if required)
- □ Ground pepper (to taste – I like lots)

And then in another bowl make a mixture of the hard stuff:
- □ I use two large packets (about 600–700g) of Tesco plain smoked mackerel. Skin the mackerel and break into tiny bits with a fork or scissors. Then add:
- □ Capers (to taste – at least half a small jar)
- □ **Lemon zest** (half a small lemon is enough)
- □ Spring onions, split lengthways and sliced fine (I use about 6; include the green bits to at least halfway up the stalk)

Now this is *very important*: add the soft mixture to the fish mixture, **not the other way around**. Put in only enough to bind and make it a good, rough consistency. If you add the fish to the sauce you might find you have too much sauce and there is no way to fix it! Make this a day ahead of time and chill overnight for flavours to blend.

(WORKS WITH SEA TROUT, SMOKED SALMON, ETC.
AS WELL)

This is a great first course but also works well with drinks. Serve it with toast triangles; cut the crusts off and slice diagonally into quarters.

If you are going to serve this as a first course at lunch, it goes nicely on the plate with some redcurrant jelly and a small salad with French dressing. I like a bit of butter as well on the plate or platter.

This is one of those recipes where the more you make it, the more you will know what to do next time to make it suit you. The proportions are not exact – you can add or subtract to suit your own taste.

VEGETABLE BAKE

You can use a variety of vegetables. Fundamental basics include:

- ☐ Onions
- ☐ Courgettes
- ☐ Carrots (roll sliced)
- ☐ Celery
- ☐ Peppers

Depending on what else you are serving or what is on hand, or your mood, you can add:

- ☐ Sweetcorn
- ☐ Mushrooms
- ☐ Leeks
- ☐ Garlic
- ☐ Potato if not being served elsewhere

Cut everything into chunks, basically fork-size – I cut the onion into fourths and separate the layers. Slice the garlic. Make sure everything is dry. Toss it all in a bowl with 1–2 tablespoons of olive oil – just enough to coat everything, no more, as you don't want this to be greasy!

Put it all in a baking dish. Make between a half and 1 cup (120 to 240ml) of **bouillon (I use Marigold Swiss Vegetable Bouillon Powder – which is a miracle product in itself)**. Make it extra strong (twice the suggested strength as there is lots of water in the veg) and pour over the vegetables.

Lastly, top it off with grated cheese – I use a mixture of Cheddar and Parmesan.

Bake for 30–45 minutes in a medium oven depending on how you like your veg done.

As you can tell this is a recipe that is not precise – you develop it as you go along and the more times you make it, the more it will suit you.

ROAST CHICKEN

Select a medium-size roasting chicken with good overall colour.
Remove any leftover bits inside and pull out any fat left in the
cavity. Use this fat to coat the breast and the bottom of the pan
you will use. Cut off the tail. Insert two bay leaves, each with a
single clove stuck through the leaf, into the cavity. Also insert two
garlic cloves (not peeled). Let the chicken sit until it reaches room
temperature.

Set your oven at 190°C or use the AGA top-right oven for the
first stage. Place the chicken **breast side down** in the heaviest
ovenproof frying pan or skillet you have. You can use a roasting
pan, especially if you are roasting two or three chickens, but the
frying pan makes better gravy.

Roast the chicken for an hour (for average size; adjust time up or
down accordingly) without turning or basting. Remove from the
oven. For the next stage, turn the oven down to 150°C and leave
the door open for one minute or use the bottom-right AGA oven.
Turn the chicken over onto its back. You can baste with pan juices
if it looks dry but this is usually not necessary.

Roast for another hour (adjust according to size) **breast side up**
and remove from the oven. If using an AGA, place the chicken on
a serving platter and put it into the plate warmer (bottom left, not
the upper-left simmer oven) to keep it warm. If you have only one
oven, put the chicken on a warm platter, cover with aluminium foil
and keep in a warm spot.

Pour all the fat off the skillet. Use white wine (I save leftovers
for this) to deglaze the skillet. If you like thin gravy, season to
taste and that's it. If you like thick gravy put 1 heaped and 1 level
dessert spoon of corn flour into a cup (240ml) of cold water. I add
the salt and pepper here, too, but until you learn how much you
prefer, do that separately. Mix the flour and water very well with
a fork or whisk and then add to the gravy. If it gets too thick, add
more wine or plain water.

Roast chicken can be served with 'Lea's Mashed Potatoes' (see
recipe on page 253), steamed potatoes or oven-roast potatoes –
it's your choice.

This method gives a nice golden-brown colour, the standing makes the meat easy to slice, and the gravy is great due to the pan juices that have burnt on to the skillet.

One of the major tricks of this is to learn to adjust the cooking time for the size of the chicken. The only way I know how to do this is from experience.

LEA'S OVEN-FRIED CHICKEN
(If you are counting calories skip this section)

I buy whole fryers and cut them up – you need a very sharp knife and a fair amount of muscle. (Try to get someone else to do it!)

I cut off each wing, leg and thigh, then separate the leg and thigh, cut off the back and divide into two pieces. I then split the breast piece in two and then split each half in two again. This gives 10 pieces of chicken per fryer. Depending on the size of appetites, you can figure that this serves 3–4.

Clean each piece well and pat dry with kitchen roll. Make a mixture of flour, salt and pepper and put in a paper bag or a bowl as you like. Lea likes a bowl, I like a bag. Flour each piece thoroughly.

Get the grease hot in the roasting dish before putting the chicken pieces in (this can be done on a ring if you have gas, but the cooking is done in the oven). Use vegetable oil not olive oil and then place the chicken in the pan. I always put it in bone side down first if there is a choice.

The oven should be at a minimum of 190°C and I fry up to 250°C, depending on the oven and how much chicken I am frying (the AGA's top-right oven is perfect). You have to use judgement and experience on this.

The secret is to fry slowly and turn often. If you have more chicken than fits in the grease at one time, you have to stack it up at one end and fiddle it about so all the pieces get at least one turn in the grease.

I would say the whole thing takes about an hour from the time you start cooking but, again, you will have to use your own judgement – with a hot oven and not much chicken it can be ready much sooner.

You can tell if it is done by inserting a paring knife into a big piece and telling by the feel.

One important technique is to **fry the chunkier pieces first** and then add in the slimmer ones, so breasts, thighs and possibly legs first, wings and back, last. This way, the big pieces are cooked for a little longer.

I like to experiment with herbs in the flour but Lea likes it better with just plain salt and pepper.

Now for the gravy (which is the real reason for fried chicken in the first place!).

When you finish frying, wrap the chicken in aluminium foil, turn off the oven and put the chicken in the cooling oven so it will stay warm or, if you have an AGA, cover and put in the plate warmer.

Pour off the vegetable oil you used for the frying (save it for the future or put it in the rubbish in a suitable container). The pan should be left with a sticky brown crust. This is what makes your gravy.

Start by thoroughly deglazing the pan. Normally I use wine for deglazing but for fried chicken gravy I use **water**. Then mix up about a cup (240ml) of water with 2 tablespoons of flour (I use the flour left over from the chicken flouring) plus salt and pepper. Add this plus a couple of cups of semi-skimmed milk. I think semi-skimmed or whole milk makes better gravy than skimmed.

From here on in you stir a lot and taste a lot. As you need it, add more milk. Also, you may need – again, depending on quantities – another tablespoon of flour mixed with cold water to add to the thickening.

Chicken gravy should be light creamy beige in colour and have lots of little brown flecks in it. Don't be afraid to add more salt and pepper to get a tang.

Obviously, this needs to be served with 'Lea's Mashed Potatoes' (see page 253)!

BARBECUE SAUCE

This sauce is ideal for ribs (pork or beef), chicken or pork chops.
It can be used on the grill outside or for oven roasting in the
wintertime.

The recipe is 'loose' in the sense that exact proportions or
ingredients are not necessarily required, and the proportions and
contents can be altered to personal taste. The end consistency
should be more runny than tomato ketchup and thicker than
single cream.

Mix all the ingredients together in a large mixing bowl. Purée
in a blender for best results but if you don't have one, or can't
be bothered, chopping up very fine or shredding will work well.
All quantities are approximate.

This will make enough for 2–3 chickens cut up into small
pieces. Mix:

- ☐ 1 large onion, puréed or shredded fine
- ☐ 2 garlic cloves, pushed through a garlic press
- ☐ 1 cup (240ml) of olive oil (plus another half-cup if needed)
- ☐ 1 cup of tomato ketchup
- ☐ 1 large can of tomato paste
- ☐ Worcester sauce
- ☐ Soy sauce
- ☐ Salt (to taste)
- ☐ Celery salt to taste
- ☐ Pepper (to taste)
- ☐ Chives/garlic chives, finely chopped
- ☐ Italian/flat-leaf parsley, finely chopped
- ☐ 2 dessert spoons of brown sugar (possibly more after tasting)
- ☐ Juice of 1 lemon
- ☐ Vinegar (apple cider is best)
- ☐ Balsamic vinegar (to taste)
- ☐ **Lemonade, Sprite or Coca-Cola** (to taste and consistency)

Paint a thin coat of the sauce on the chops, ribs or chicken pieces
a couple of hours before grilling: this will allow the flavour to seep
in. Then, while cooking over a low grill heat, keep brushing on the

sauce lightly. Watch to avoid burning as the sugar in the sauce can turn to charcoal.

It is best to cut up the chicken into the *smallest possible* pieces for really juicy grilling. If you grill big pieces, they can get too done on the outside and not done enough on the inside. Each side of the breast should make 3 pieces, each leg and thigh 2 pieces.

BAKED BEANS
(From scratch)

Serves 6 – this recipe is easy to multiply for as big a pot as you like.

This recipe was originally published by *Gourmet* magazine in the United States over 50 years ago. Everyone says they are the best baked beans ever. They take a lot of time but the results are very much worth the effort.

Pick over 2 cups (480ml) (400g) of haricot beans or pea beans carefully to remove any bad ones and then put them in a pot with 4 cups of cold water (960ml) to soak overnight. The pot should be kept in a cool place. In the morning, the beans should have absorbed most, if not all, of the water. If any water remains, drain it off and reserve it.

Add fresh cold water to the roasting pot or pan, tightly cover and simmer the beans over low heat for an hour. (After the first 10 minutes, remove the lid and skim off the scum and any beans that have floated to the top.)

Put a 4oz piece of salt pork or fat bacon in the bottom of a big earthenware bean pot or heavy roasting pan and pour in the beans.

Bury a second piece of salt port, weighing about 8oz and well scored, in the centre. Mix together half a cup (120 ml) each of dark treacle and reserved bean water or plain water if no soaking water is left, 1 tablespoon of dark brown sugar, 1 scant teaspoon of grated onion, half a teaspoon of dry mustard and quarter of a teaspoon of paprika. Pour the mixture over the beans, lifting them carefully with a spoon so that the seasoning will penetrate to the bottom of the pot.

Cover the pot and bake the beans in a slow oven (140°C) for 6 hours. Once each hour, add a little of the reserved bean water, again lifting the beans gently so that the water will sink to the bottom of the pot. The surface of the water in the pot should always just cover the beans. If there is too much water, the beans will stew instead of baking, and if there is too little water, the beans will become dry and hard rather than tender and mealy.

During the last hour of cooking, remove the lid of the bean pot so that the surface will become crisp and brown.

I have had good luck with this recipe for picnics, multiplying it up to the size of my biggest roasting tin.

DEVILED EGGS
(Nebraska style)

Boil a dozen or two-dozen eggs until they are hard (at least 20 minutes).

After they are completely cool, crack off the shells and slice in half lengthwise with a sharp knife.

Put the whites on a platter and pop the yolks out carefully into a mixing bowl.

Thin some mayonnaise with cream, add salt and pepper, prepared mustard, and **the secret ingredient (gherkin juice)**. Mix this in with the egg yolks until you get a fairly stiff mixture.

Reload the eggs with this mixture. Place on a cold platter and garnish with chopped parsley and a little paprika.

These are great with drinks in the summertime and as a garnish with cold salmon.

After you make these a few times you will learn how much mustard and pickle juice you prefer.

COLD POACHED SALMON
(Lord Suffolk's foolproof method)

Use a 4–5lb salmon, whatever will fit comfortably in your fish kettle. (You can't make a whole poached salmon properly without a fish kettle!)

Plan to cover it with court bouillon and white wine. Use Sancerre, another Sauvignon Blanc or whatever you can bear to spare – at least one bottle. The poaching will probably take at least four bottles of court bouillon, which I make as follows:

COURT BOUILLON:
- 4–6 wine bottles of cold water
- 1–2 leafy stalks of celery
- 2–3 tsp of salt
- 2 small carrots or 1 large carrot, sliced in half
- 1 medium-size onion with 6–10 cloves stuck in it

- ☐ Several stalks of parsley (use the stalks and leafy parts for flavour)
- ☐ 2–3 bay leaves
- ☐ 12–20 peppercorns, bruised
- ☐ 2–3 slices of lemon including the rind

Simmer the above for at least half an hour (an hour is better). Then cool it down completely by setting outside or adding a few ice cubes.

POACHING THE SALMON:
All the ingredients must be completely cold for this to work! Put the salmon in the kettle and cover with the court bouillon and wine as per above. If you are a bit short, add water and be more careful to make enough next time!

Bring the salmon to the boil with the lid off. Watch it very carefully. After it starts to boil, time it for **EXACTLY ONE MINUTE – NO MORE!**

Shut off the fire (or remove from the heat), cover the kettle and let it stand until it cools down to almost room temperature. The cooking takes place while the water is coming to the boil and after you have shut it off. The size of the salmon controls how long it takes (i.e. how much heat) and this process governs the cooking perfectly.

After the salmon has cooled, set it outside in winter or in the refrigerator in summer (still in the kettle covered with the cooking water) until it is completely cool.

SERVING:
After it is completely cool (probably the next day) drain off all the liquid. Place the salmon on a platter on lettuce, rocket or watercress, and skin the top side from behind the head to just before the tail. Replace the skin with paper-thin slices of cucumber as scales, starting at the head and working down.

Serve with mayonnaise or yoghurt sauce flavoured with dill. Devilled eggs (see previous page) are also a good garnish and go very well with cold salmon.

AMERICAN POTATO SALAD
(Great for picnics)

To make a large bowlful, boil 6–8 medium-size potatoes in their jackets. Put some bay leaves and a bit of salt in the water for flavour. At the same time boil about 4 eggs until they are hard. If you don't like the smell of boiling eggs, put a little vinegar in the water.

Peel (if you wish) the potatoes after they are thoroughly chilled, dice up into squares about three-quarters of an inch across and place in a large mixing bowl. Shell the eggs, crudely hand-chop into chunks and add.

Cut 2–3 stalks of celery into half-inch chunks and add. Take a jar of gherkins and chunk up 4–5 to taste, and add in.

Then chop up a medium-size onion and put that in as well.

The dressing is mayonnaise thinned with a little milk. Flavour it with prepared mustard (American or French, not English) and then **take 2 teaspoons of the juice from the gherkins** and add to the dressing as well.

Season the mixture well to your taste and then add the dressing.

Chill in the refrigerator for about 4 hours before serving.

For lunch, it is best to make the potato salad the day before. For dinner, make it in the morning. It saves well in the refrigerator for a day or two and it's better to make it too early than too late as the flavour improves as it chills.

You can mix in a bit of parsley and/or chives for flavour and also sprinkle some chopped finely on the top for presentation, and dust with paprika for colour.

CORNWELL CAKE
(A great way to use up leftover roast potatoes, the crispier the better)

Serves 2–4 depending on serving size desired.

Put equal parts of olive oil and butter in a large, flat, heavy skillet (I find that this dish works best in an omelette pan). Cut up the leftover roast potatoes into small chunks – no more than half an inch diameter. Toss in the potatoes when the grease gets hot and brown them.

While the potatoes are browning, you should stir them once in a while, and also make up your favourite scrambled egg mixture.

In this case, use about 4 eggs depending on size. Add salt and pepper to taste and then add a little milk or water as desired to scramble. Beat up well with a whisk.

Arrange the potatoes evenly spaced over the bottom of the pan. They should now be pretty crispy. Add some butter to the pan and pour the egg mixture on the potatoes carefully so it covers the pan.

Let the eggs cook for a while without disturbing them and, as the mixture begins to firm, slip a spatula under and loosen it up. After it is loose, shake the pan from time to time.

After the mixture starts to brown around the edges, indicating it is almost cooked, slide it onto a plate as big as the skillet. Make sure the skillet is still greasy so the eggs won't stick and invert it over the plate held in one hand. Hold the two together face to face and flip them over so the undone side of the cake is now face down in the pan.

Finish off cooking, which should only take a few minutes, then cut up and serve.

MUSHROOM SAUCE
(Ideal with steak)

This mushroom sauce is easy to make and is ideal with grilled steaks.

For 6–8 people start with a 1½lbs of fresh mushrooms, whatever kind you like. The better they are, the better the sauce.

In a large, flat, heavy skillet, melt equal parts of butter and olive oil. Sauté a handful of chopped shallot and one bunch of spring onions sliced halfway up the stalk so you get some green as well.

When the onions turn clear, add the mushrooms. I use large ones and slice them into cubes about three-quarters of an inch square. You can use little ones whole if you prefer.

Boil a cup (240ml) of water and add two beef OXO cubes (or use leftover beef gravy).

When the mushrooms start to cook down, add in the beef stock and a handful of chopped parsley or chives or a mixture of the two.

Use leftover red wine to add as you cook the moisture away. If you are so inclined, a finely pressed clove of garlic adds a nice touch. Add salt and pepper to taste.

As with any sauce that contains fat and water, the risk of separation is always there. I find that constant stirring is the answer. If the sauce cooks down too much, you can add more red wine at will. In fact, I find the sauce is better if it requires 2–3 additions of red wine to keep it the right consistency.

ST MORITZ FRENCH TOAST

I stayed at the St Moritz Hotel in New York for several years and was always in love with their French toast. They never would give me the recipe but after years of trial and error, I think I have almost got it:

To serve 4 people, you will need:

- ☐ 1 egg
- ☐ 1 egg yolk
- ☐ ½ cup (120ml) of cream
- ☐ 4 tbsp **sweet sherry** (Harvey's Bristol Cream is good)
- ☐ 2 tsp vanilla extract
- ☐ Salt
- ☐ Caster sugar
- ☐ Ground cinnamon
- ☐ Butter (unsalted is best)
- ☐ Sweet syrup (maple is best)
- ☐ Stale bread

Make a cinnamon and sugar mixture, about a third cinnamon and two-thirds caster sugar. I keep mine in a large chef's salt shaker.

If the bread is not completely stale, stale it by putting in a moderate oven for half an hour or leave it out with the pieces spread out overnight. The more stale the bread, the better the toast. The bread can be of any type but it is best cut diagonally into half slices.

In a medium-size mixing bowl mix the egg, the egg yolk, the cream, some sherry, a teaspoon of sugar, a pinch of salt and the vanilla extract, whisk it up and see how the consistency is. If it is too thin put in another egg but it will probably be too thick; if so, add just enough milk to get the right consistency, which is about that of single cream.

Melt some butter in a large, flat, heavy skillet and, when it starts to sizzle, dip the bread in the batter long enough to coat but not become soggy and fry until crispy. After turning, dust with the cinnamon and sugar mixture so lightly that you can't even see it on the top.

Serve immediately on a hot plate with maple syrup.

LEA'S MASHED POTATOES

For enough to serve approximately 6 people, wash and peel 6 large, 12 medium or 18 small potatoes.

Boil in a large pot with a thick bottom, along with 3 dried bay leaves, a medium-size onion **and a handful of chopped celery including plenty of leaves**. Salt the water.

While the potatoes are boiling, heat half to 1 cup (120–240ml) of milk.

When the potatoes are thoroughly done but not overcooked, remove from the heat and drain. Return the potatoes to the heat and shake the pan, or alternatively place the pan in a moderate oven for a few minutes to be absolutely certain all remaining water is removed.

Mash the potatoes in the hot pan. Return to mild heat and add 2 tablespoons of butter and the hot milk until you get the desired consistency. I mash with a heated-up hand masher and stir in the butter and milk with a wooden spoon.

Adjust the seasoning with salt and pepper. If appearance is important, use white pepper.

Mashed potatoes hold beautifully if covered with a teacloth and placed in the warming oven. Do not put on a lid or they will steam and lose their texture quickly.

The combination of flavours, onion, bay and seasoning make these mashed potatoes delicious with or without a gravy or sauce.

If you are feeling brave or healthy, you can try leaving on the skins.

TACOS
(With sexist comments concerning serving size)

This recipe makes more than enough for 2 (as long as they are not teenage boys) and might work for 3 (as long as only one of them is a teenage boy).

Buy the following from El Paso, which is the best brand available in most supermarkets:

- ☐ Packet of 12 taco shells (hard corn tortillas)
- ☐ 1 jar of mild salsa
- ☐ 1 packet of taco spice mix
- ☐ **1 can of refried beans**

You will also need:

- ☐ 500g of high-quality lean beef mince
- ☐ Lettuce of your choice (anything but iceberg)
- ☐ 20–30 small tomatoes (I like the flavour of Tesco Finest Vine Ripened)
- ☐ 240g sharp Cheddar (Cathedral City or similar)
- ☐ Sour cream
- ☐ 1 medium-size onions, 2 cloves of garlic, dried oregano and thyme

Chop the onion finely and sauté in a small amount of olive oil until clear; about halfway through add the chopped garlic and some oregano and thyme. When clear, take the onion and garlic out of the pan and brown the mince. Meanwhile, stir half (no more) a packet of taco spice into 125ml of warm water. When the mince is brown (fully brown for best flavour) return the cooked onion/garlic to the pan and add the taco spice liquid, and stir. If you need more liquid use red wine. When the beef, onions, garlic and spice are fully mixed and **before all the juice cooks away, add a third of the can of beans**, stir in and mix thoroughly. Heat and serve the rest of the beans on the side if you like that sort of thing.

While all the above is cooking, chop a pack of tomatoes (20–30 little ones) into quarters, grate the Cheddar and chop up 3–4 big handfuls of chopped lettuce.

When ready to serve, heat the taco shells in a very hot oven **for 3 minutes** – no longer as you want them warmed not toasted.

Put 2–3 rounded tablespoons of the meat mixture into the bottom of each shell (I serve 3 shells for girls and 4 for boys), sprinkle cheese on top of the meat, then add tomatoes and cover with lettuce – by now the shell should be overflowing.

Finish with a dab of salsa and a dab of sour cream on each taco. Serve immediately.

It is possible to eat these with your fingers if you are in private and near a shower but a knife and fork won't go amiss.

I would be amazed if your guests did not come back for seconds.

Have plenty of napkins handy!

ONE LAST NOTE

In the above recipes I have put certain things in 'bold' typeface. You might wonder why I did this. As discussed throughout the book, retailing is about getting all the ingredients and the timing and the proportions right. It is about quality and about presentation.

But there is one more thing to remember . . .

After you get all the 'basics' right, what is the MAGIC ingredient that makes your shop or your website 'special'? What makes it different from the others – like the olives in the Bolognese sauce, the celery in the mash or the cognac in the chicken liver pâté?

To really excite and delight customers there has to be something unique and special about what you deliver!

ABOUT THE AUTHOR

John Hoerner has been a successful retailer for more than 50 years. His work has taken him from Hovland-Swanson speciality store in Lincoln, Nebraska, where he started work in 1959 while still at university, to Woolf Brothers speciality store in Kansas City, followed by Hahne's in New Jersey, H. & S. Pogue in Cincinnati and L.S. Ayres in Indiana, three divisions of Associated Dry Goods subsequently acquired by May Company and now part of Federated Department Stores.

In 1987 he was recruited by the Burton Group to run Debenhams, a chain of 59 department stores in the UK. Debenhams grew and prospered over the next five years to become one of the most profitable groups of department stores anywhere, and in 1992 John was made Chief Executive of the parent company with over 2,000 stores in the UK. In 1998 John led the demerger of Debenhams from the Burton Group, which made substantial returns for shareholders compared to the share price when he became Chief Executive.

The remaining chains of multiples were renamed Arcadia Group, which John ran until 2000 when he retired from Arcadia. In 2001 he joined Tesco, the world's third largest retailer, based in the UK, to lead the development of their clothing business. In 2006 he took on another Tesco assignment to consolidate the clothing businesses in Central Europe and Hungary, the Czech Republic, Poland and Slovakia, which all joined forces to develop a powerful business. Since 2008, John has been a consultant for Tesco, helping the development of Tesco clothing in China, Korea, Thailand, India, Malaysia and Turkey.

John is a keen pilot, a hobby that he put to good use visiting stores during his career in the UK. He was a trustee of the London Battersea Dogs & Cats Home for 19 years, 7 years as Vice Chairman and 4 years as Chairman. He served for three years as Chairman of the British Fashion Council, which sponsors London Fashion Week. John lives on a farm in Gloucestershire with his wife Lea, their three horses, and their five rescued dogs from Battersea Dogs & Cats Home.

Acknowledgements

So many people have helped me throughout my career that it would be impossible to name them all but Clarence Swanson and Jim Swanson at Hovland-Swanson in Lincoln, Nebraska, Jim Wallis at Woolf Brothers in Kansas City, Herb Yalof at Hahne & Co. in New Jersey, and Red Largay and Bill Arnold at Associated Dry Goods stand out as significant contributors to my success in the USA. At Debenhams and the Burton Group Sir John Hoskyns was a great mentor. At Tesco, we could not have achieved what we did without the support and coaching from Richard Brasher, John Gildersleeve and Sir Terry Leahy.

When it came to writing the book, I owe a lot to my friends and colleagues who gave me valuable feedback on the very early drafts. Julia Cook, Shelly Sams, Terry Kugrens, Philip Clarke, Amanda Kearns, Weike Pan, Lina Roh and Georgia Coleridge were incredibly helpful.

I cannot forget to mention all my supplier friends who over the years taught me the value of doing business with the right people.

The Chinese version of this book published in July 2015 was made possible by the dedicated help as Weiping Luo and Jenny Qi. Mr Yao, Mr Huang and Mr Yi from Guangdong Economic Publishing House developed the creative idea of both a Chinese and English version sold together as a pair.

When it came time to publish the UK/USA English version Ebury Press led by Carey Smith, Publishing Director had the confidence to take on the project, which was greatly enhanced by superb editing suggestions from Lydia Good and Howard Watson.

I have received so much help from so many people during my career that my purpose in writing this book was to help others who choose retail as their career choice. Hopefully, those who take the time to read this book will find at least one or two ideas that make it worthwhile.

John Hoerner